CONTEXT IS EVERYTHING

FOR TOM

W. H. FREEMAN AND COMPANY
NEW YORK

SUSAN ENGEL

# CONTEXT IS EVERYTHING:
## THE NATURE OF MEMORY

TEXT DESIGN: VICTORIA TOMASELLI

The following permissions to quote have been granted: *The Treatment* by
Daniel Menaker, ©1998 Daniel Menaker, by permission of Alfred A. Knopf
Publishers; *Treating Troubled Adolescents* by H. Charles Fishman, ©1988
H. Charles Fishman, by permission of Basic Books; "Still Alien, Still Angry,
Right Mom?" by Rick Lyman, July 11, 1997, *The New York Times,* ©The New York
Times Company, by permission of The New York Times Company; *Oleander,
Jacaranda* by Penelope Lively, ©1984 Penelope Lively, by permission of Harper-
Collins Publishers; "All Our Yesterdays" by Jorge Luis Borges, translated by
Robert Mezey and Dick Barnes, translation ©1995.

**Library of Congress Cataloging-in-Publication Data**

Engel, Susan.
    Context is everything: the nature of memory/Susan Engel.    p.    cm.
    Includes bibliographical references and index.
    ISBN 0-7167-2997-0
    1. Memory.    I. Title.
BF371.E535    1999                                          98-51361
153.1'2 – dc21                                              CIP

Printed in the United States of America

First printing, 1999

W. H. Freeman and Company
41 Madison Avenue, New York, NY 10010
Houndmills, Basingstoke    RG21 6XS, England

# CONTENTS

Preface   vii

Chapter 1   Where Memories Begin   1

Chapter 2   Memories Created in Conversation   24

Chapter 3   Courtrooms and Therapy Rooms   52

Chapter 4   Then and Now: Creating a Self Through the Past   80

Chapter 5   Remembering in Print   109

Chapter 6   Laying Claim to the Past: When Memories Become History   146

Notes   170

Index   181

# PREFACE

In Jorge Luis Borges's marvelous and strange story, "Shakespeare's Memory," the main character is a dusty pallid scholar of Shakespearean literature. While attending a conference, he goes one evening to a bar where he meets a man who gives him Shakespeare's memory. The scholar is ecstatic, believing he has just received the key to his fame and fortune. What more could he wish for than literally to possess the memory of his intellectual idol? Instead, though, he finds himself overwhelmed with the burden of recalling Shakespeare's memories. He has inherited, along with scenes and events from Shakespeare's life, the guilt and worries that accompany them. Ultimately he cannot bear it and rids himself of Shakespeare's memory by giving it to someone else.

To try to imagine, fully and specifically, what it would be like to borrow someone else's memory forces one to confront essential questions about the nature of remembering. Can a memory travel from one person's mind to another? What might this transfer involve? In what ways are memories borrowed, exchanged, and transformed in everyday life?

Recently I found myself in a heated discussion with my sister about a long-ago party at which the hostess forgot to serve birthday cake for her husband, the guest of honor. I remembered the occasion in vivid detail. It had a long-lasting effect on me (at the moment of the discussion we were making a cake for the same guest, who had gone without cake all those years ago). As I was going on, reminding my sister of details from that distant evening—what we had eaten for dinner, what the hostess had said, how people had responded to the lack of a birthday cake—my sister suddenly turned and looked at me skeptically. "You weren't there. Don't you remember? I went to the party without you, and called you up for a cake recipe hoping I could make one quickly to remedy matters." I had remembered her memory. Yet even now that I know it didn't happen to me, I continue to recall it as if I had been there.

The experience of recollection can be extraordinarily powerful. The personal, internal strength of a moment of remembering is only matched in force by the interplay between people when they exchange memories. Sometimes the communication and use of a memory are at odds with the internal experience of the past. But those two domains of experience—personal/internal and public/external—form the two axes along which memories are made manifest.

In recent years the topic of memory has become so popular, it seems both ubiquitous and yet oddly invisible. People glide seamlessly from a discussion of childhood recollections to national memories, as if they were part of the same phenomenon. I would like readers to identify the process of remembering where they haven't noticed it before. And at the same time, I hope readers will gain a more delineated picture of what memory is and isn't in various contexts. Part of what I have learned over the years in gathering material and data on memory is that in most settings the participants who are remembering are also defining memory for each other, or in Erving Goffman's fortuitous phrase, "creating a frame." I hope the book argues convincingly that memory between two intimate friends is a different animal from memory in a courtroom. A moment of vivid re-experiencing is, by the same token, altogether a different enterprise from a written autobiography. Through all these contexts bubbles the problem of truth. What is an accurate memory, what is not, and when does this even matter? Truth, like memory itself, is a notion that often only becomes palpable in the interactions that unfold between people.

A smart friend once told me to write the book I would like to read. When I started this book, what I desperately wanted was a way of thinking about memory that would help me sort through the magnificent but bewildering array of studies and insights that have emerged over the last 10 years. What are the theoretical connections that link these studies together, and along what lines might they be contrasted with one another? This book represents my attempt to write the book I have wanted to read—to construct a framework for thinking about memory.

Many helped me with the ideas and material in this book. To begin, I thank my cherished adviser and first editor, Jonathan Cobb. Years ago he introduced me to the expression "ur." He is my "ur" editor. The following people contributed, knowingly or unknowingly, to the ideas presented here: Lucy Prashker, Scottie Mills, Jenno Topping, Kathy Engel, Tinka Topping, Herman Engel, Al Goethals, Katherine Bouton, D. L. Smith, Liz Coleman, Susan Borden, Ave Schwarz, Margery Franklin, and the marvelous students who have taken my courses in memory and autobiography over the last several years, at Bennington and Williams Colleges.

I would like to thank my editor at W. H. Freeman and Company, John Michel. We got to know each other literally over the pages of this manuscript. He is a pleasure to talk to and work with, and has given me unflagging encouragement and great advice along the way.

I would also like to thank Amy Trask, whose interest in the substance and details of this book was so helpful.

Finally, of course, I thank Jake, Will, and Sam Levin. They are enthusiastic, tolerant, interested, and supportive of my work. And they are an unending source of my best memories.

CHAPTER ONE
# WHERE MEMORIES BEGIN

Every September, just as the days begin to end at 7:00, my grandmother says, in her lazy, comfortable voice, with a touch of whimsy and a touch of pragmatism, "Jack Frost is coming soon. One of these nights he's going to get out there with his paintbrushes and start painting the leaves." I don't know which is more startling, that I still believe her or that she's been dead for 13 years. As when I was 7, I believe her against my better judgment. When I was little, wan, and blonde, with hair that alternately swung in a chic pageboy and hung limp and straggly, we'd sit at her kitchen table eating toasted Wonder Bread spread with oleo. I already knew, by then, how an IUD worked and what method acting was. But when she warned me of the coming artistry in the trees, I could feel and see Mr. Frost gaily dancing out in the clear dark of a September night, leaping delicately from branch to branch, capriciously touching up the leaves, tossing out an endless splash of orange, red, yellow, and dark purple. Even now, at 38, when my grandmother has been long dead and I have children far older than I was when I first learned about how the leaves got their fall color, I feel the same irresistible pull to see it as she said it.

Looking back, I grasp what I didn't fully understand then, or perhaps with the bifocal view of childhood I did understand—that she was delighted by the image, tickled to tell me. But it didn't sound fanciful. It sounded like the plain truth the way she said it: "This is how things work."

I walk along my driveway with a son or two running, or hopping, or dragging beside me. I have just gotten the mail, or picked some tomatoes, or stolen some wine from my mother-in-law, who lives next door. I am thinking about whether my 13-year-old should go to boarding school. I am thinking about why certain people I work with are depressed, or cautious, or dull, or all three. I am thinking about how to begin my next chapter. Whatever it is I am thinking about, suddenly my grandmother Helen will begin speaking. Her voice has the same inexplicable southern lilt it always had (inexplicable because she spent every one of her 76 years on the eastern end of Long Island). As I walk up the driveway, I am distracted by her voice in my ear, and the fleeting glimpse I catch of Jack Frost as he disappears into the trees.

Next, I see her hands. She was beset by frailty all through her adult life. There was much more she couldn't do than could do. She couldn't get my breakfast, she couldn't manage real grocery shopping, she couldn't keep her house clean, she couldn't read a whole book, she couldn't be loving to both her sons, she couldn't make it to Sunday services at her beloved Methodist church. She couldn't even drive up the street for the Sunday paper. Once I could reach the gas pedal, at 11 or 12, I drove, and she sat next to me, fat and soft with a house dress and unhooked bra over huge, pendulous breasts. (We'd park on the side street so the policeman wouldn't see us, and I'd run in and get the paper. I tried to convince her to read the *New York Times,* but she didn't want it. Just the *Daily News* and its funnies. We'd both wear nice underwear because she always reminded me that if we had an accident we wouldn't want the emergency workers to find us with ugly panties.)

She was weak, but her hands were strong. Meaty even. With cuts and marks, war wounds from planting a geranium in a teapot, mixing strawberry Jell-O and fruit she had made for me, preparing bones for the lumbering black dog named Bear (actually, my stepfather and his brother called her Bear, we ladies called her Cindy). At the slightest nick, deep red blood would gush from her. This was a sign of robustness, we agreed. All the competence that was missing in the rest of her life gently radiated from her hands. She smelled of Bengay and talcum powder.

Sometimes I would spend the night. I'd lie in the same soft bed in which my stepfather had lain as a boy. I thought the softness was the ultimate luxury. A sign of a special night. My mother told me that the best beds were hard beds; only uneducated people chose soft beds. After I'd pee ("Do you need to use the terlet?" she'd ask), my grandmother would sit by the bed to kiss me good night. She barely concealed her perpetual shock that I chose to sleep naked. But even so, she'd say the Lord's Prayer with me. So there I lay—naked, thin, wallowing in the guilty pleasures of an overly soft bed—a precocious, agnostic Jew, 7 years old, recounting the Lord's Prayer with my grandmother. Once I came into her room in the morning to wake her up, and to my repulsed and fascinated surprise, found her teeth sitting in a glass next to her bed. Only uneducated people had false teeth, my mother said. Perhaps my grandmother sensed this and felt ashamed. As my eyes landed on the teeth (and no doubt widened), my grandmother quickly and delicately took the edge of her pink candlewick bedspread and draped it over the glass.

I am saying too much. I cannot recount everything about my grandmother. Nor would I tell you even if I could. I can only admit that when she speaks to me, I listen with the same longing I did then. And I still don't quite know what it is I long for.

Every memory journeys from its first vivid moment within a person to its multifarious transformations and uses within the world. After this unexpected, unsearched-for memory and the thoughts and feelings that come close on its heels, the memory's fate is uncertain. Will it wash away, a passing moment in my mental experience never to be recalled? Will I talk about it to someone else? Will I publish it in a memoir? Will its telling elicit a family argument about whether I really said prayers at my grandmother's house? Will it hurt my stepfather that I think his mother was frail? Or change the way he remembers her? (My mother says, upon reading my recollection, "I didn't say uneducated people had false teeth, I said people with no money got false teeth.")

Whether a fleeting image or an historically situated autobiography, each memory rests, in some way or another, on the internal experience of recollection. Much of the time these internal representations are surprisingly accurate and provide us with rich sources of information. Scientists now know more than ever about the precise ways in which our memories can also confuse us. The mental procedures involved in putting together a scene from the past rest as much upon constructive processes as they do upon retrieval.

In his short story "In Dreams Begin Responsibilities," Delmore Schwartz describes a 21-year-old man imagining his parents' courtship. The young man sits in a movie theater watching his parents, as young lovers, on the movie screen. The description of his young father and mother is so detailed, so vivid, you forget that you are reading about a character imagining this scene. And then, suddenly, the 21-year-old character who is telling the story jumps up to cry out and warn his parents not to get married, knowing as he does that their future will be hateful. An old woman sitting next to him in the imagined movie theater chastises him for making noise, suggesting he get hold of himself. At this point in the story it is hard for a reader to disentangle the writer from the character, the present from the past, and the future of the two young lovers that has since unfolded. The kaleidoscopic sense of past, present, and future experienced in one person's mind as a topsy-turvy sequence of insights and images captures the way our memories often function in everyday life. Moreover, Schwartz's strange twist, in which the most private reverie is made public, points to a real aspect of everyday remembering. Others—by invitation or intrusion—often end up privy to what we recall, and what we think of what we recall.

What appears in Schwartz's story as a literary and crafted view of the complex and jumbled nature of memory, reflection, and prediction of the future touches on a truth that psychologists are only beginning to dissect in research. Many scholars have recently pointed out that memory is not one process but a constellation of processes. In *Searching for Memory*, for example, Daniel Schacter has shown that memory depends on a variety of neural activities that converge to create recollective experiences. Much of how and what we remember depends on a host of factors: how intact our brain is, the specific clue that triggers a particular search for memory, how old we are, how we took in, or encoded, the information or experience in the first place, how much time has elapsed since the original experience, how frequently we have recalled the memory, and what we are doing and feeling at the moment of recall. These are just some of the factors that influence the quality and precision of a particular act of recollection.

Recent studies have shown, for example, that when people suffer damage to the hippocampus (and connected areas of the medial temporal lobes) they will find it almost impossible to recall specific events but seem able to learn new skills. On the other hand, patients whose basal ganglia have been damaged suffer the opposite symptoms: they can recall specific events but cannot learn new skills. The more we learn about the physiological underpinnings of memory, the more we see the complexity of the processes involved. Coordination between processes is clearly a requirement of such a multilayered phenomenon.

There are several layers of the phenomenon we refer to as memory, and recent years have brought great advances in what we know about almost all of these layers. Here is a thumbnail sketch of those layers. Several parts of the brain have been identified for their role in one kind of memory or another. In addition, we now know that people build up neural pathways for memories, and that the more often that particular memory is invoked, the more solid and strong that neural pathway becomes. We also know that the neural mechanisms that lead to memory are very similar to the neural mechanisms used for imagining things. This has suggested to some that there is a physiological basis for the complex interweaving of fact and fiction in people's personal recall.

Many people use a computer metaphor to describe the sequence involved in remembering. This sequence has been quite useful in identifying developmental and individual differences in recall behavior. The metaphor comes from information processing and the early days of artificial intelligence. Therefore, psychologists tend to think of memory as occurring in three stages: input, storage, and output. When you take in an experience, the form and organization of that input have a strong impact on how, how long, and how well you will recall something. For instance, you can recall something as an image or a story. You can organize a series of items in groups or as a random list. You can tag something in terms of its relationship to similar events or experience it (and tag it) as a unique event. All of these variations have to do with the input stage of remembering.

The next stage of remembering—storage—remains, by and large, the big black box of memory research. Somehow, events we have experienced remain in our minds. It is hard not to have a physical metaphor for this. We think of memories as pictures in a file box, or complex networks of sentences. We know bits and pieces about how memories work during what's known as the storage phase. For instance, we know that memories one uses often tend to be recalled better than those to which one rarely refers. The exceptions to this are traumatic or vivid memories that may be revisited internally (rehearsed), but remain private and unspoken for years. Finally, there is some evidence, though controversial, that memories can remain repressed, unavailable to consciousness, and then resurface 20 years after the fact.

Scientists still don't know exactly what it means to say that a memory stays in the brain. And this brings us to the third stage in the memory process—retrieval or output. Twenty years ago, psychologists tended to think of retrieval in terms of the way a computer works: you use some sort of search cue (a time, a key word, a title) and find the memory waiting in some corner of the brain, in somewhat the way you might use a word to search for a document in your computer files. Research has now shown that, instead, retrieval is almost always more a process of construction than one of simple retrieval. One creates the memory at the moment one needs it, rather than merely pulling out an intact item, image, or story. This suggests that each time we say or imagine something from our past we are putting it together from bits and pieces that may have, until now, been stored separately. Herein lies the reason why it is the rule rather than the exception for people to change, add, and delete things from a remembered event.

Researchers don't yet fully understand the rules that guide this construction process. Something is known, however, about the kinds of situations and cues that facilitate and hinder remembering, or retrieval. One key element in this phase of remembering concerns possible matches between the way material is elicited and the way it might have been encoded in the first place, or stored in the interim. One classic method of finding out how people organize material in memory is to give them lists of items in differing kinds of groups and find out what type of grouping promotes or hinders recall. For instance, when young children are given a list of items, they use no special organizing principle to recall the items. When they are asked to recount what was on the list, they give disorganized and random recounting of the list, and usually recall few items. On the other hand, older children will immediately group the items into categories. So, if the items on the list are orange, hat, scissors, knife, shoe, shirt, shovel, apple, bananas, hoe, pants, and cherries, older children and adults are likely to recall it in the following way: orange, apple, cherries, shovel, knife, hoe, scissors, hat, and pants, thus demonstrating something about the way they grouped the items. Moreover, if prompted with categories—fruit, tools, clothes—children who haven't spontaneously organized the items will be helped by the labels. In this way, researchers have experimented with material that subjects are asked to recall, and they tinker with the cues they offer those subjects. The thinking goes like this: if specific manipulation of the material to be remembered makes people remember more quickly, or more accurately, we can assume that our manipulation in some way matches the internal organization that people are using either at the time experiences are encoded or at the time they are retrieved.

Researchers have also found it extremely useful to group memories into different categories. In the most famous and long-standing conceptualization of memory, suggested by Endel Tulving in the 1960s, people are considered to have two kinds of memory: semantic and episodic. Semantic memory refers to things you recall without any sense of when you learned them or when you experienced them. It is a timeless sort of memory, more often thought of as knowledge. For instance, you probably know where you lived as a 5-year-old. But when asked where you lived then, you readily access the information as a kind of ongoing knowledge rather than a specific event that occurred at a certain time or in a certain place. Similarly, you know how to do all kinds of things without knowing how you learned them or when you learned them. I know very specific things about planting flowers and vegetables, learned as a child, but I cannot locate a specific time or occasion on which I learned how to make rows in the dirt in a particular way. The memory of planting guides my actions but is not available to me as a memory to muse over, or even describe. We all know vast quantities of information about places and people without any sense of a particular event, or even a time when these things were learned.

On the other hand, there are all kinds of memories that are remembered as having happened in a particular time and place. The time I almost drowned in the ocean, the day I defended my dissertation, the moment I gave birth to my first child. These memories come tagged with information about when and where they happened.

As with so much else about memory, real life is seldom as clear and well defined as the research describes it. Many memories are a blend of episodic memory (something that happened in a certain time and place) and semantic memory (timeless knowledge). For instance, I have a very specific memory of reading *Wuthering Heights*. I had a serious sunburn while on a family vacation when I was 13, and I spent two days in a darkened hotel room reading while everyone else was out on the beach. I also have a lasting and now timeless knowledge of what is in the book *Wuthering Heights*. However, my memories of that first reading are deeply intermingled in mood, look, and emotions with the story that Emily Brontë told.

Scientists also differentiate between short-term memory and long-term memory, though what most people mean by these terms and what a psychologist or neuroscientist might mean differs. Researchers consider short-term memory to be very short indeed—things that happened in the last few minutes. The time that lapses between hearing a phone number from a friend, hanging up the phone, and dialing that new phone number would be considered short-term memory. Anything that moves much beyond this time frame (recalling a breakfast conversation at dinnertime) becomes long-term memory. A great deal of information that is stored for mere moments is then lost forever. Most of us, however, think of short-term memory as the things that have happened in the last hours, days, and weeks. Anything beyond this, we think of as long-term memory.

At each point in the memory process, and with each type of memory, researchers have now identified a host of factors that influence the memory. To give just a few examples: the mood you are in at the time of recall; uniqueness—you are more likely to recall things that stand out (climbing to the top of a mountain) and will find it difficult to remember events that were one of many (Christmas dinner when you were 7); frequency of recall—if you have recalled an event time and again you are more likely to remember it than if you have never thought or spoken of it.

Some aspects of the memory process are the same for everyone. Almost everyone remembers his or her own role in past events as being more central than it really was, for example, and most people recall things more firmly when they have repeated the recollection over time (otherwise known as rehearsal). Other aspects of the memory process, particularly what it feels like to recall the past, seem to function in a more idiosyncratic way. For instance, one woman who is writing her memoirs says that her memory of each year is shaped like an egg. December is at the top, the spring and summer months at the wide middle, and autumn at the bottom. As she looks back on any given year, she finds (or constructs) an episode by first locating its place on the egg. Clearly, this is a distinctive way of thinking about and experiencing the process of recollection. And while the underlying neural processes may or may not reflect this idiosyncrasy, nevertheless her subjective experience of remembering is individual. If we are ever to construct an adequately dynamic and integrated picture of how memory works, we need to know much more about the links between the experience of remembering (what people can say about how it feels to remember) and less conscious levels of functioning (the neurology of remembering, social influences, etc.). More and more research has demonstrated that when it comes to psychological processes, our stance toward the process and our conscious belief about what we are doing and why affect the mental activity itself. In Ann Brown's groundbreaking work, she showed that one of the most important developmental changes to occur in childhood is the deliberate use of strategies to aid memory, dubbed meta-memory. To take another example, research on cultural differences in how people organize knowledge shows that people employ different patterns of organizing information depending on what they think the purpose of the task is. The implication of these findings for autobiographical memory is that how we think about what we are doing may well influence the way our mind carries out the process of remembering.

Although the experience and physiology of these private internal moments of recollection are fundamental to understanding the process, most of the kinds of memory that we encounter in daily life go far beyond the intimate personal re-experiencing of something from the past. Much of our remembering involves public transactions of one kind or another. For example, we tell a group of friends about something we did years ago, or testify in a court of law about something we saw happen weeks earlier. By public transactions, I mean all the ways in which we share, negotiate, and present our memories to other people, including collaborating with others in the construction of a past event. The moment that an internal image, sound, smell, or scene is told to another person, it becomes a new phenomenon, emerging from, but not confined to, an internal image or scene. Once we recall with or for others, the process of remembering depends as much on motivation and social context as it does on any neural network.

In the last 20 years, researchers have gathered a great number of pieces of the puzzle of memory. In both theory and controlled experimental settings, researchers have drawn a picture of how the pieces come together. What we don't yet know is what happens to these pieces when they converge in real-life settings. The elements that form a model of memory in an experiment may interact quite differently to form the live, shifting, and vivid experiences we know as memory. Of particular interest is the way in which these factors express themselves in the complex and potent settings that involve other people. Between the folds of one's mind and the expression in words or pictures of a memory lies a process of manifestation that is extremely complex but worth understanding. The pieces of this process, such as the form of information when it is encoded, the construction and strengthening of neural pathways, and the effects of damaged ganglia, only begin to cohere when we think of them in terms of their expression in real people and in real lives. This argument is akin to the one made by the genetic biologist Richard Lewontin, who feels that genetic messages (such as the information regarding a person's intellectual capabilities) can only be understood in terms of their expression in a real environment. One's capacity to function at a given intellectual level is only meaningful in relation to the social environments in which one develops and uses one's intellect. To take another example, Lewontin refers to the enzyme defect that leads to phenylketonuria (PKU). Children born with this recessive hereditary disease predetermined by their genetic code suffer brain damage and mental retardation if they are exposed to foods containing phenylalanine, such as dairy products, but *only if* they are exposed to phenylalanine. In a similar way, the process of remembering can only be understood in an appropriately rich and dynamic way if it is understood as a kind of chemistry between inner processes and outer settings. It is the dynamic interplay between inner and outer that gives rise to the thing we know as memory. Another geneticist, Claudio Stern, puts it this way:

> Learning about the genome for its own sake as a means of understanding biological processes is like learning a language by memorizing a dictionary. . . . You have all the pieces but you are missing the rules. This does not mean that the dictionary is useless. But when do you come to understand the system? Is it when you understand all the components or understand how the components interact?

The minute I talk about my grandmother, my memory of her undergoes transformation. The first and most obvious change is that what I might have experienced as nonverbal sensation or a visual image must become, de facto, a verbal narrative. To even tell you, my reader, about her, I have to put her into words. I have to sequence my memories of specific events, mark them temporally, give the memory a grammar, and structure it in a variety of ways that let you know it was me experiencing something from my past, not to mention conveying to you what it was I am experiencing from my past. Try this with one of your own unexpected private and vivid memories. If you are good with words, film, or painting, you may capture a great deal of what you originally experienced. Nevertheless, if you pay close attention, you can see that this is a different process from the original private one. What may have been inchoate becomes sequential. What was fleeting takes on substance. What might not even have been clearly marked as a memory now becomes embedded in grammar that marks it as something remembered, something from the past.

As memories make their way from the inner reaches of our minds to the world of conversation, books, therapy, and history—and back again—the already layered processes involved in producing mental experiences of the past become embedded in several new layers of social life. Why am I recalling my grandmother? With whom am I talking about it? Did they know her or participate in the events I describe? What are the consequences of remembering some particular event with her? Will it give me new status, challenge someone else's self-image, implicate someone in a wrongdoing? All features of the context in which I recall her now play a formative role in the memory process.

Autobiographies present an intriguing example of the possible changes that a memory undergoes as it travels from the personal to the public. Take any of the most poignant or vivid moments in well-known autobiographies. These literary moments are often precise, and evoke the sensations we all associate with private internal memories. In her lovely memoir of growing up in Egypt, *Oleander, Jacaranda,* Penelope Lively recalls traveling as a little girl in a car outside of Cairo, saying over and over again, "Jacaranda, Oleander, Jacaranda, Oleander," mesmerized by the sounds of the words. It is the kind of snippet from the past that brings with it a flood of connected feelings and ideas. Lively has captured not only a familiar quality of childhood, but also what it feels like to revive momentarily a vivid bit of one's own past life.

Contrast Lively's vivid memory crafted into a piece of literature with the following recollection. Startlingly succinct, sensuous, and evocative, it emerged in a completely different context. In a fascinating project run by a psychologist and a writer in New York City, people with Alzheimer's disease meet every other week to write about their past. After much hesitation and scratching out of words, one participant, 69-year-old Elizabeth Mudd, writes: "I remember picking a fig from a tree in Athens. My lover watched me with delight." Mrs. Mudd said of what she wrote, "That's the wonderful thing—it comes from somewhere if you let it. It was a small thing but it said all it needed to. That was in the 1950s. That's exactly what happened. It was quite a love." In both cases, one by a polished writer, the other by someone with strikingly diminished mental skills, the essence of an experience is captured perfectly and evokes in the listener not only the substance but the feeling of the person's past. Both also convey a bit of the feeling of the recollective process itself.

By the time a snippet like Lively's is included in a published memoir, it is no longer simply a memory but a work of art, a piece of something larger—a deliberate act of self-presentation and communication. The memory now entails much more than the actual momentary experience of the rememberer. In her precise and evocative account of her childhood, *The Liars' Club,* Mary Karr describes a searing episode in which an older neighbor sexually abused her. The detail is mind-boggling, and must involve as much imaginative creation as it does accurate recapitulation. What we hear of Karr's childhood is as much a function of her narrative skills and her motivations in writing the book as it is a function of her actual recollections. As so many memoirists have said, one has to sift through the facts to get to the real story. In order to evoke certain feelings in a reader, or make clear a particular theme, the writer transforms, adds, and deletes from what might have started as a raw and inchoate memory to tell a story.

What comes out as a memory in conversation or writing may take on a story form through the process of expression or communication. At the same time, our recollections are often elicited by and formed with other people. When this is the case, the past is created through narrative rather than being translated into narrative. For instance, if you are sitting among a group of friends who are reminiscing about their first kiss, you may recall an episode you have never consciously thought of before. Not only do other people direct you to this memory, the process of telling stories with these friends may literally guide your search for the until-now-forgotten kiss and shape your construction of that moment long ago.

Think back to some charged event in your own life. Perhaps the first fight you had with your spouse. Now imagine telling that story to your mate, many years later at the celebration of your twenty-fifth wedding anniversary, telling it to the divorce lawyer, telling it to your children now that they are grown up, writing it in a humorous memoir of your now famous life, or telling it to your therapist. In each case the person you are telling it to, and the reasons you are telling it, will have a formative effect on the memory itself.

A devastating and profound example of both the differences and the deep connections between the internal individual experience of the past and the public uses of the past is presented in Tom Segev's *The Seventh Million*. In this account of the politics of people's memories of the Holocaust, Segev shows how people's strong, detailed recollections of life during the Holocaust not only shape the rest of their lives but, taken together, form the basis of a whole nation's cultural and historical identity. The personal recollection is the tangible and powerful experience upon which much larger, more conceptual histories are built. (Chapter 6 will expand on the notion that individual memories are changed as they are gathered and reconstructed for shared purposes.)

## Telling the truth

In the recent outpouring of memoirs, autobiographical writing, and psychological investigations into the reliability of memory, there has been tremendous focus on what it means to tell the truth about the past. This concern is most evident in the reactions to memoirs of childhood trauma, as well as legal proceedings based on recovered memories. A careful exploration of memoirs, literary writing about autobiography, and psychological experiments on memory suggests that telling the truth about the past means different things in different situations. Our implicit, everyday criteria for truth vary as a function of the purpose for which we are using memory. But this tends to be a somewhat invisible aspect of the memory process, overlooked as often by psychologists as it is by the people doing the remembering.

When alone (on a walk, in a car, in the bath), or even possibly with a therapist, a memory is true if it resonates with oneself, illuminates one's life, and affords a sense of continuity and identity to the rememberer. In his marvelous memoir, *My Last Sigh*, Luis Buñuel writes,

> In this semiautobiography, where I often wander from the subject like the wayfarer in a picaresque novel seduced by the charm of the unexpected intrusion, the unforeseen story, certain false memories have undoubtedly remained, despite my vigilance. But, as I said before, it doesn't much matter. I am the sum of my errors and doubts as well as my certainties. Since I'm not a historian, I don't have any notes or encyclopedias, yet the portrait I've drawn is wholly mine — with my affirmations, my hesitations, my repetitions and lapses, my truths and my lies. Such is my memory.

But once a memory becomes public and is used for any of a variety of social purposes, people hold it to a somewhat different set of truth criteria.

For example, take the newly celebrated author, Kathryn Harrison. Her memories of her psychologically and sometimes physically absent mother and incestuous father take on a whole new significance now that she has published these reminiscences in *The Kiss*. Among other things, these memories now become accusations that have implications for the lives of others. What might have been considered true simply in some emotional sense within the context of therapy (what Donald Spence has called narrative truth) now must be held up to what some call consensual truth. Do others agree that she recalls it accurately? What effect will her public use of this memory have on members of her family? If one remembers something incorrectly but privately, it is far different from remembering incorrectly and publicly. What was purely subjective and only as true or untrue as the insight it afforded the rememberer might now be viewed as a delusion or a lie.

Consider the example of David, a middle-aged man, who remembers an awful and damaging childhood. His version of his past, told to therapists, siblings, friends, and his own nuclear family, is rich and compelling. The description is cohesive, filled with affect and detail—all characteristics of a truthful childhood memory. And in one way, his memory is personally truthful—providing insight for him. As Buñuel says, it is the sum of his errors and doubts as well as his certainties. But at some point, David's version of his past has begun to turn on itself, and failing to free him, it instead has enslaved him. His past has become a source of laying blame. He has used his recollection of an unhappy childhood as the basis for waging a kind of war with several members of his family, and also as a rationale for his own dysfunctional behavior. He argues that he must keep secrets from his mother because he learned as a child he cannot trust her. Thus he explains the secrets he has kept from her in running the family-owned store. He claims he was never valued as a child and thus must take money from the store because his mother cannot acknowledge his worth. At some point he began to use his version of the past to control and convince others about current events. A private experience of the past became a public use of the past.

What is striking, but familiar to anyone who has discussed their own childhood with their siblings, is that David's four grown siblings recall things very differently. While David recalls his mother as cold and withholding, his sisters and brothers recall her as warm and present. This in itself could be the kind of difference in recollection you would find among any group of adult siblings. Under the best of circumstances, these versions coexist. Siblings accept that either the reality was different for each child (the mother behaved in fundamentally differing ways toward each) or one could conclude that the filter of looking backward has wrought differently toned stories for each. That is, siblings recall the basic elements similarly, but have imbued these memories with differing intensities and shadings of affect. The siblings could shrug and agree to disagree. But when one sibling uses that kind of recollection to shape current events, including influencing practical decisions (in David's case, the management of family finances), what it means to tell the truth about the past goes beyond the realm of subjective or narrative truth. In David's case, recollection of a painful childhood has become the pedestal on which all his current rage sits. It confirms and strengthens a view of his mother that puts him into conflict with her and works to distance him from his siblings. The more disparate his view is from that of his four brothers and sisters, the more emphatic about his memory he becomes.

This last feature is one of the intriguing characteristics of the memory process. David's memory feels just as real to him as the siblings' memories of the past feel to them (and would feel that way whether the mother treated them quite differently or not). As is so often the case, the accuracy of a memory does not correspond to the vividness of a memory. In a classic example of this, the distinguished memory researcher Ulric Neisser describes his long-standing clear-as-a-bell memory of when he heard that Pearl Harbor had been bombed. He was in his living room listening to a baseball game on the radio when the announcer broke in. It was only years later (in middle adulthood) that he realized this was impossible. No major league baseball game would have been played in December. The feeling of clarity of a memory has no reliable correspondence with its accuracy.

Psychologists now understand more about how this kind of mistake can happen. It turns out that people commonly suffer from what is known as source amnesia. We have a vivid memory but don't know what its source is. So, for instance, people forget which part of a story they tell came from something they read and which part came from firsthand experience. Studies show that after people are shown a short video of an event and are subsequently given written versions of it that contain false information, for instance, they are likely, when asked to describe the event, to include information from the misleading written narratives. They could not differentiate between what they had seen in the film and what they had read in the story.

In another study of source memory, adults were given a list of names that included those of famous people (for example, Ronald Reagan), along with made-up names (for example, Sebastian Weisdorf). Several minutes later, when asked to comment on the list, they could easily distinguish the famous names from the fictitious ones. The next day, however, when those same subjects were asked to look at the list they were likely to claim that many of the fictitious names were familiar and probably famous, though they already had forgotten the source of their familiarity with the fictitious characters.

Such examples all suggest that as time goes on, we repeat a story to ourselves and think of it as our memory. It is the norm rather than the exception to be unable to distinguish between what happened, what you feel about what happened, and what others may have said about what happened. Moreover, these studies show that there is little correspondence between what feels vivid and accurate and what is accurate according to an objective or consensual account of events.

## When public shapes the private

When a memory takes on a public form it doesn't necessarily lose its internal psychological intensity, but it may subtly transform it. In fact, sometimes the public use of a memory gives it a definition and substance it didn't have when it lived only in one's mind as a fleeting and infrequent visitor.

Once you've shared a memory, the internal memory you store is influenced and sometimes merged with the version you shared. A 9-year-old girl comes home from a basketball game, head down, feeling devastated. The game went badly, and she missed the last shot that could have won the game. She tells her mother how badly she played, how miserable she feels. The father walks in from the car and says to the mother,

> You would have been so proud. Simone was a hero. If it weren't for her the team would have given up in the second quarter. But she wouldn't let them stop trying. In the end she missed the last shot, but if it hadn't been for her, the game would never have ended as close as it did.

The next day Simone tells a friend at school,

> It was a pretty good game. We lost, but not by much. The other kids wanted to give up after the first half. But I wouldn't let them. It's a good thing. This way, the score wasn't so bad at the end.

Over time, Simone's memory will be of that shared version of the event, not the version with which she began. The psychologist Elizabeth Loftus has shown, in fact, that young children can come to remember events that never happened. In a now famous study youngsters were induced to recall being lost in a mall when in fact this was not the case. Leading questions and suggestions by an older peer or an adult helped the children to create an experience that they became convinced had actually happened.

This kind of situation, in which people subtly change the past in response to an audience, happens all the time. A colleague tells the following story:

> We took our 9-year-old son to have his tonsils out in day surgery. I was tense and miserable seeing him in such discomfort, sad and guilty that at his young age he had already undergone so much surgery. When he came out of the operating room he was all hooked up to I.V.'s and other tubes, moaning and writhing. I went to lie down with him and put my arms around him in his cot, getting all tangled up in the wires. I began to laugh wildly at the absurdity of our situation — my silly tangle in the wires in contrast to his misery and the depressed and serious atmosphere of the recovery room. I found in the months and years that followed, when I told my friends about the experience, this moment of hilarity became the focal point of my story. I guess I thought it made the story entertaining. But I think I probably liked this view of myself — you know, the mother able to laugh in any situation. Now, 4 years later, that is all I can remember of the episode.

Changing a memory to please an audience and then having that shape the memory is only one way other people influence our recollections. Neisser has shown in several studies that the social significance of an event influences how well, and what, we recall of that event. In a host of studies on the emergence of autobiographical recall, researchers have shown that when young children recollect out loud, it may best be viewed as a kind of performance. The context in which they perform with their memories influences the development of the remembering process. When young children recall an experience from their past, they are apt to do so with the help of others. This is one of the ways in which the social context—the public uses of memory—interacts with the private experience of the past.

A large number of studies have shown us the ways in which people are likely to distort memories. Some researchers, such as the social psychologist Shelley Taylor, have argued that many of these distortions help us to maintain a positive self-image and a happy outlook. In fact Taylor refers to these as positive illusions. Other researchers, most notably those from a psychoanalytic perspective, have tried to show that repression and distortion keep us from living as fully conscious and happy lives as we might.

## Negotiating the past

Once a memory is made public, the possibilities for disagreement, persuasion, and consensus become a dynamic part of the psychological process of remembering. Take, for example, the case of Henry, an elderly man. Henry, his grown daughter, Katherine, and her son Timothy all participated in an event that had a completely different fate in the memory of each person. None of them would have even known this if it had not become part of a subsequent argument.

The argument concerned how the three interacted in making vacation plans for Timothy to visit his grandfather, Henry. In a heated exchange, both Henry and Katherine recalled a similar tension 3 years earlier. They agreed that that episode had been the precursor to this current tension, and they both recalled it as significant. But they remembered startlingly different versions of it.

Henry's version:

> I remember it very clearly. Timothy was all excited about his idea to take a trip to Madrid with us. He was running up to you [Katherine] with a paper on which he had written down what we could do on the trip and when he could go. You waved him away, very tense, saying, "I am much too upset about this to discuss it with you."

Katherine's version:

> Henry and Timothy sat at the table excitedly planning a trip to Madrid, oblivious to the fact that Timothy's brother was sitting nearby, hurt that

he was left out of the plans. My father and Timothy came over to me completely focused on their idea, wanting to discuss possible travel dates. I was very irritated that my father, Henry, the adult was so unaware of how this made the younger brother feel, and also angry that he was encouraging Timothy to get excited about a big trip without first discussing it with me, since I'm the mother. In the middle of cooking, cleaning, and caring for everyone I certainly wasn't about to sit down and figure out the logistics, nor was I going to get into a long discussion about the problems of leaving the younger brother out of the plan. So I said, "I can't really discuss this right now."

Timothy's version:

I wanted to go to Madrid. Grandpa was very excited about the idea and we started planning it. When we went over to Mom to discuss travel dates, she said we'd have to discuss it later.

This case illustrates two points. First, people can disagree about almost any level of a given memory: detail, meaning, sequence, or even whether the event happened at all. We have come to know better what those different levels are and what causes us to remember one level versus another. What has received less attention, but is equally important to a full understanding of this pervasive and essential phenomenon, is the way in which a memory like this is not only a psychological entity within a person but a social transaction between people. In the case of Henry and Katherine, the vehemence with which they present their memories to one another, the particular differences they each insist on, their willingness or refusal to blend memories, and the emotional consequences of the memory transaction are a central part of understanding their memories. The developmental psychologist Peggy Miller has shown that young children who recount past experiences to their families derive two kinds of emotional mileage from sharing their recollections: the re-experiencing of whatever they felt at the time of the event and the emotions that result from sharing the episode. They have the opportunity to cool a painful experience by putting it in a story form, analyzing it and attempting to understand it, or get over it by retelling it. They also get to try and elicit sympathy and support from their listeners. Miller argues that this accounts for her subjects' predilection to tell stories of personal hardship and woe.

The examples of Simone's basketball game and Henry's plans to travel with Timothy show how people construct the past in the company of others. Sometimes features of the larger context also direct the way a memory is constructed. In the following two examples, subtle cues that come from the setting itself direct the rememberers to relate the past to the present in very particular ways.

Lauryn is a patient in a psychiatric ward. She is there because of severe postpartum depression following the birth of her first child. In a family therapy session the social worker asks her about her childhood. Lauryn grew up as the second eldest of four children. Her father was a dairy farmer and her mother a housewife who suffered such severe depression that when Lauryn was little her mother had received electroshock therapy. By all accounts the father was a stern and unyielding man. During the present therapy session Lauryn is trying to communicate how repressive her father's exacting standards were. She says,

> I remember this one time when he told me to stack the wood. When I was done he came over and restacked all of it, because I hadn't done a good enough job.

Lauryn is using a memory from her past to illustrate an emotional theme that is at this point timeless. It has more to do with an ongoing quality of her father's relationship to her, and her experience of that, than it does with any one episode. And yet clearly the story has come to exemplify the theme, or hold it in some way. She may have told it many times by now, each time using it as a way of letting others know something about what she experienced, as well as who she is now.

By contrast, Perry, an ex-convict who is now a counselor for male convicts, is talking to other counselors about how he got in trouble in the first place. Perry explains,

> I think I had loving parents. But once, when I was 10, I did something bad. I can't remember what. And my parents sent me to my room for a period of time. I can remember everything about that day. The way the bedspread looked, what was in the room. And I remember that it was there and then that I decided my parents didn't love me. From then on, for the next 20 years, I knew they didn't love me.

This is a strange story. Something is not right about it. What Perry wants his listeners to believe (and no doubt he himself believes) is that his parents were loving, but that the one punishment erroneously convinced him they didn't love him. He uses this as a way of explaining the subsequent years of juvenile delinquency. In this case, an anecdote is not used to give a sense of drama and vividness to an ongoing life theme. Instead, the event itself is seen as having caused a subsequent life theme. Moreover, his claim that his parents almost always acted lovingly seems doubtful. If, in fact, they behaved in a loving and accepting manner most of the time there is little likelihood that one punishment could have made him believe otherwise or caused the deep emotional problems he claims were precipitated by the punishment. A memory of an event that may serve as a template for a larger theme in his emotional life is recalled instead as a specific cause of subsequent problems in his life.

In this case, an individual attributes a lifelong emotional difficulty to one isolated event, insisting it caused, rather than captured, the nature of the problem.

Lauryn and Perry are good examples of two people using childhood memories in two very different ways. The first is what I have described as a template memory, one that communicates, for the self and other, a larger more timeless issue in a person's life. The second is represented, no doubt incorrectly, as the catalyst that shaped the next 20 years of a man's life.

## The consequences of remembering

Why does it matter that anyone remembers his or her past correctly? How do we balance our insight that memory is subjective with our need to know when memories are true and when they are false? In *The Naked Heart,* Peter Gay examines why the bourgeoisie of nineteenth-century America and Europe were so absorbed with autobiography. He points to the Victorians' celebration of the individual, and with it a focus on the idea of the self. This focus drew them into a fascination with the internal life of individuals. Their preoccupation was the precursor to the contemporary sense that subjective experience is of paramount importance, and sowed the seeds of our current distrust of objectivity. In the twentieth century we have taken the obsession with subjective experience, the individual, and the power of inner life to new heights. At the same time, paradoxically enough, we have become increasingly concerned with facts, tests that purportedly can get at the true status of something (one's genetic makeup, one's intelligence, one's honesty, etc.). Our thinking about memory reflects perfectly this seemingly contradictory love of the subjective inner life and dependence on an ability to get at the objective facts that explain the world.

Autobiographical memory is on the one hand a deeply personal, subjective, and vivid construction of the past, a construction that reveals, creates, and communicates a personal identity. But we constantly use these memories in public transactions. To that extent we expect reliability, accuracy, and objectivity. What and how we remember has consequences for our own lives and the lives of those included in our memories.

It is not only in the fall that I think of my grandmother. Thoughts of her come back to me all the time. Mostly they are deeply private. I see the Sunday paper, and the word "funnies" flashes through my head. I smell a certain kind of talcum and I instantly see her bathroom again. I hold a wooden spoon a certain way, and can feel her tutelage in my hand. But these moments and flashes are evanescent and fleeting unless I share them. There are stories that I have shared—so often they have lost their feeling and sense. They have become shells. But sometimes a deeply felt moment or scene from the past rises up from the past that lies dormant in my brain and finds its way outward. These moments, where past meets present, where the inchoate finds form, where the rememberer finds a listener, are the ones that demand insight and understanding.

I toast a slice of Sara Lee pound cake for my 11-year-old son and butter it. Just the look of the hot butter sinking into the cake evokes my grandmother. Handing the plate to him I say, "I used to eat about 10 slices of this for breakfast at my grandmother's house. I'd spread the slices with oleo. Mmm, they were delicious. Sometimes I'd lounge around her kitchen for hours toasting and buttering pound cake." As I say it, I can feel a long nascent sense of languor and well-being wash over me. My son squints his eyes a little and tilts his head, as if to say, "You? Lie around eating pound cake?"

Now the memory of my grandmother has a whole different structure and a new purpose. Now it has a life outside of my thoughts. Among other things, it is now part of my son's memory of me, and gives him a new trajectory in his representation of me. I have offered him a view of me as little, indolent, and piggy. Now that I have spoken of my grandmother to my son, and written of her in a book, my private images of her have also been transformed. There are new rules and consequences to this now public and formed memory. Once shared, a memory is changed forever.

My goal in this book is to draw lines of connection between the inner, private experience of personal recollection and the social transactions that shape so much of our everyday uses of memory. Inherent in this effort is an attempt to understand what it means to tell the truth about the past, and how truth criteria differ from one situation to the next. The act of remembering draws on myriad convoluted and powerful processes. Equally complex and essential to human experience are the ways in which we use our memories, both alone and with others. The private internal dimensions of remembering and what we do with our memories deeply affect one another. This book is the story of that interpenetration.

# CHAPTER TWO

# MEMORIES CREATED IN CONVERSATION

## From within to between people

My 12-year-old son is asked to describe an important memory for a class writing assignment. He sits down to write it, looks up at me, and asks, as if it were the most reasonable question in the world, "Mom, what is my most important memory?" Why does he assume that anyone can know his memory, much less what particular memory might be most important to him? He assumes this because he knows implicitly that relationships (such as his and mine) rest on shared memories and that, conversely, memories grow out of what happens between people. As Rainer Maria Rilke wrote, "Memories, many of them not my own, are passing shyly and vividly though my chamber."

## Remembering as an act of intimacy

Much of the time, in fact, there is a fluidity between what is internal and what is shared that can be confusing. While the internal experience of a personal memory can be intense and have deep and lasting ramifications in one's life, most memories have some realization in the world of social transaction. The force of conversation (interaction) can be as powerful an influence on what is recalled as the force of the past.

People do not as a rule construct autobiographies or even autobiographical pieces on their own. Most of the time, anything more than a fleeting remembrance of a moment from the past happens with others (for instance, in conversation) or is constructed for others (for instance, in the form of writing).

One of the most charged ways in which people use remembering is as a route to intimacy. In one of the great love scenes of all time (in Leo Tolstoy's *Anna Karenina*), the hero, Levin, breaks through his own constraint and the misunderstandings of the past and reaches out to the young woman he loves, Kitty Oblonsky. They are at a dinner party, seeing each other for the first time after a long separation that followed on the heels of a sad and tense parting. It is nineteenth-century Russia, and Kitty is seated at a card table covered with green cloth. She is talking to Levin about the nature of arguing, distractedly drawing lines on the cloth with a piece of chalk. Afraid that their conversation is rapidly coming to a close and that she will leave, Levin takes up the chalk.

> "Wait a minute," he said, sitting down to the table. "I've long wanted to ask you one thing."
>
> He looked straight into her caressing, though frightened eyes.
>
> "Please, ask it."
>
> "Here," he said; and he wrote the initial letters, w, y, t, m, l, c, n, b, d, t, m, n, o, t. These letters meant, "When you told me it could never be, did that mean never, or then?" There seemed no likelihood that she could make out this complicated sentence; but he looked at her as though his life depended on her understanding the words. She glanced at him seriously, then leaned her puckered brow on her hands, and began to read. Once or twice she stole a look at him, as though asking him, "Is it what I think?"
>
> "I understand," she said, flushing a little.
>
> "What is this word?" he said, pointing to the n that stood for never.
>
> "It means never," she said; "but that's not true!"
>
> He quickly rubbed out what he had written, gave her the chalk and stood up. She wrote, t, l, c, n, a, d . . . .
>
> Kitty, with the chalk in her hand, with a shy and happy smile looking upwards at Levin, and his handsome figure bending over the table with flowing eyes fastened one minute on the table and the next on her. He

was suddenly radiant: he had understood. It meant, "Then I could not answer differently."

This is the moment of discovery for Kitty and Levin. Their ability to clarify what has happened in the past and to convey to one another their experience of that past in code captures the essence of their love and tells them they are in fact meant for each other. Though it is said that this incident really happened between Leo Tolstoy and his wife, Sophie, it also captures the romantic fantasy most of us have, that a mere lift of an eyebrow tells a whole story to the one we love. In Emily Brontë's *Wuthering Heights,* Cathy Linton can only express her complete and devouring love for Heathcliff by saying, "I am Heathcliff." But in fact, the more substantive exchanges that help people become close are the revelations they make to one another regarding information about themselves—autobiographical information. Some of the most powerful, quintessential love scenes in novels occur when the writer evokes the eros and passion that emerge as lovers tell one another about their lives. In Boris Pasternak's great love story, *Dr. Zhivago,* while staying together in an isolated country house, Yuri begs Lara to tell him about her life. Nothing could be more ardent than his request to hear the details of her past. He wants to know her by knowing what has happened to her.

## The earliest remembering couples

The urge to connect through the past, to tell what the other doesn't know about your life, as well as revisiting what you experienced together in the past, is a cornerstone of most kinds of intimacy, and has its roots in what Daniel Stern has called the first relationship. Stern, a researcher and clinician who has studied mother-infant relationships for over 25 years, has shown that mothers and their babies are engaged in an intricate exchange of intimacy that literally resembles a dance. Videotapes show that mother and baby closely follow and match one another's gestures, words, intonations, and gazes. He calls their ability to gauge one another and respond in kind "attunement," and claims that successes and failures in this attunement reflect the quality of the relationship. As the title of one of his most well-known books, *The First Relationship,* implies, he believes that patterns of future relationships are often formed through this primary one. Almost anyone, however remotely influenced by Freud's views on early life or by John Bowlby's view of attachment, would agree with Stern in viewing the early mother–child relationship as a pivotal influence on the course of a person's later relationships.

Many developmental psychologists believe that the early years exert strong, albeit sometimes complex and subtle or even unpredictable, influences on later life. One of the domains that researchers have spent a good deal of time and thought on in the last 10 years concerns the developmental origins of memory. As researchers in general have started to pay more attention to the role of culture and context in the development of mental processes such as language, problem solving, and memory, they have begun to see that autobiographical memory in particular begins early, and in a social context.

Specifically, during the past 15 years, developmental psychologists have paid a great deal of attention to the emergence of autobiographical talk. Many, myself among them, have argued that personal memory only really takes shape when toddlers are talking with others, most often their parents. The most extreme form of the developmental argument is that early reminiscing begins as an interpersonal process and only becomes intrapersonal over time. What begins as a social interaction between parent and child paves the way, developmentally, for the internal construction and perusal of narratives about the personal past. There is plenty of theoretical and empirical support for this view. Before examining autobiographical talk, however, it might help to locate this kind of talk in a general picture of children's early remembering behavior.

## The first signs of autobiographical memory

When a baby sees a familiar face, you can see the recognition in his expression right away. He will smile or simply begin following that familiar person with his eyes. If it is someone who typically comes up and tickles him, or in some other way pleasurably stimulates him, he may even anticipate that pleasure with wriggling or reaching. If, on the other hand, someone unfamiliar walks into the room, most babies by the age of 7 months will respond with a sudden cessation of motion, a momentary suspension of activity. A heart monitor would show a momentary change in heart rate. This tells researchers that young babies have some kind of memory that causes them to respond differently to things they have seen before. Even infants can react to an object, sound, or person in a way that tells us they recognize it.

This early recognition memory is a far cry from the long descriptions of past experience one might find among college friends or writers of autobiography. Babies cannot even say they are looking at a familiar face, much less communicate any fuller memory they might have of a feeling, an observed event, or an experience. Most developmental psychologists now agree that at the earliest phase of life we recognize things from our past, but have no elaborated recollections of experiences and events.

On the other hand, babies' memories are more well structured and complex than was once thought. By the time children are 10 months old, they react in a way that indicates that they know when a sequence they are familiar with has been changed. For instance, if every morning you take your baby in a stroller down the street and stop at a series of familiar shops, and one morning instead you walk to a park the baby has never been to, she is bound to register a level of attentiveness that shows she knows this is different. The inference researchers make from this is that in indicating her awareness of a change in a routine, she is also indicating her memory of that routine. So, in addition to being able to distinguish between isolated sounds, images, or people that are familiar and ones that are novel, babies form memories of sequences of objects, actions, and people. In other words, babies as young as a year can remember the orderly and meaningful temporal and spatial relations that occur between elements, not just the elements themselves, as we once thought.

In the past 10 years researchers have shown that one of the most primary and natural ways infants and toddlers organize and retain experience is in the form of sequences, or, as they are usually now called, scripts. The notion of scripts was first introduced by two cognitive psychologists, Roger Schank and Robert Abelson. They suggested that people spontaneously organize experiences into something like a script, with actors, goals, and actions. Moreover, they argued, people order their experiences sequentially with beginnings, middles, and ends, all organized around some clear goal. The idea is that people draw on these mental scripts as a way of organizing thought and negotiating everyday life.

The developmental psychologist Katherine Nelson used the notion of scripts to explain how children first come to make sense of everyday life. She argued that even in infancy we apprehend the world as a series of routines that we represent as scripts. So, for instance, the toddler has a breakfast script, a going-to-the-park script, and a bedtime script. Each of these scripts allows the child to know what to expect in a given experience—what will come first, who will participate, and what will happen next. Nelson's research showed that in fact children first organize a wide array of information in terms of scripts. When a 3-year-old is asked what she had for breakfast that morning, she is likely to shrug her shoulders and look vague. When asked instead, "What do you have for breakfast in the morning?" that same 3-year-old is likely to say, "First I have juice, then I have a waffle, or sometimes cereal." While the child cannot pinpoint specific information from the past, she can draw on her general scripts for experiences to access her knowledge. Nelson and a host of colleagues and students showed that over time children use these general scripts as a basis for all kinds of complex conceptual knowledge, and that in fact these scripts provide a kind of framework or background for the recollection of more idiosyncratic or special events.

Meanwhile, as a child is collecting a repertoire of scripts that represent and assimilate routines and events he has experienced, he is also learning to talk. Not surprisingly, speech plays a central role in the development of autobiographical memory. During the second and third year of life, as children begin to talk with others, one of the things they talk about is past events. In the 1960s and 1970s, language researchers focused on the child's interest and emphasis on the here and now. But in the early 1980s, psychologists began to see that parents and their toddlers were also doing quite a bit of reminiscing. A 2 1/2-year-old looks up at some adult friends and begins, "When I was just little, I went in the ocean alone. Right, Mom? And what did I say?"

Identifying important events from the past, and most significantly, doing this in partnership with a parent, turns out to be a potent form of interaction and thinking for many young children. The first studies on this topic showed that social interactions between toddlers and their mothers were the site of rich references to past events. This research was followed by a series of studies showing that the style and frequency of those interchanges had a formative effect on the child's ability and proclivity to recount the personal past. In other words, 2-year-olds need someone else to help them describe their own past experience. Parents (or other caregivers) vary in how often they bring up the past, how rich their descriptions are, and how attuned they are to the toddler's changing ability and interest in reminiscing. These features of the adult's reminiscing style all influence the child's own emerging independent autobiographical memory. In studies of preschoolers' conversations with one another about their lives and their memories, there are clear differences among the children in style and frequency of autobiographical talk. Some evidence supports the notion that shy children are less likely to engage in reminiscing with friends than their more gregarious counterparts. Other studies have hinted at the possibility that family styles of interaction when talking about the past lead to individual differences among older children.

## Language and memory: The fragile reminiscences of children

When researchers have tried to identify the origins of autobiographical memory they have often focused on the elusive question of whether children's internal representations of the past are fully reflected in the conversations they have with adults about the past. Can children remember on their own, or outside of these kinds of discussions? Can they remember only what they talk about? Do their narrative skills constrain their autobiographical memory? These are contentious issues, and hard to pin down with experimental data.

The question of what researchers are looking for, and what we measure, is as central to the debate on the origins of memory as it is in other psychological domains. For instance, 13 years ago I presented data at a conference on child development in which I attempted to convince my audience of researchers that autobiographical memory (verbal descriptions of past events and experiences) first occurred with a partner who had experienced the event with the child. I was trying to show that the memory was created between the two and was in some sense intersubjective. A highly respected researcher in memory development came up to me at the end of my talk and said that though my data were fascinating, and showed the rich interactions toddlers and their mothers had about the past, I hadn't identified what part of the memory the child had on his or her own and what part belonged to the mother. This comment reflects the view that there is always some individual internal capacity that can be assessed, separate from what emerges in the transaction between people. The researcher's remarks were disheartening to hear since the whole point of my paper had been to show that there is no meaningful representation of the past outside of the one constructed jointly in conversation. By mean- ingful, I mean something that the child can reflect on, exchange with others, or build upon. I didn't then, and I don't now, mean to say that toddlers have no independent memories of the past. The claim I was making then, and which has since been corroborated in the research of others, is that narrative descriptions of specific past experiences are first constructed with others. That is, it may be pointless to ask what part of the capacity the toddler has independent of an adult.

Obviously, the only way of knowing what children recollect of the past is through what they say about it. Yet several researchers have shown that children's ability to construct a past event in words is quite fragile. This has become a particularly relevant, if not heated, topic of concern and inquiry in light of the use of children as witnesses in sexual-abuse cases. A series of studies have shown that children who are not able to answer a question such as, "What did Sandy do to you?" can answer questions such as, "Did Sandy hurt you?" In experimental simulations in which the child's accuracy can be assessed, children as young as 3 can correctly answer the yes/no version of a question to which they cannot provide a full or even partial description. (Moreover, children are especially susceptible to the suggestions of adults who are questioning them. There are at least two sources of this suggestibility. One is that most children are eager to please an adult who is talking to them, and therefore likely to fall in with the construction of an event offered by an adult. Elizabeth Loftus's work has demonstrated this most powerfully. Loftus and her colleagues asked children aged 5 about the time they got lost in the supermarket (an event the researchers knew had not happened). A majority of the children could be led to believe this event had happened. They could be persuaded, in fact, to the point where they added details about the event and described their feelings at the time of the event. On the other hand, as Kail points out, children do correctly recognize what has happened and what has not when asked nonleading questions requiring a yes or no answer. What does all of this tell us? That the way children retain and recall information from the past changes as they develop. That before they can construct a description of the past they can respond differentially to what is familiar and what is unfamiliar. The research also shows that young children are especially responsive to and dependent on the cues and responses they get from their remembering partner. The way that information is elicited from a child has a powerful effect on their responses. Long before their narratives of the past are stable, those narratives still contain rich information for listeners and for themselves.

What is less contentious than the early relationship between language and memory and the suggestibility of young rememberers, but equally compelling, is that whether or not there is more to children's memory than what they can converse about with a partner, we do know that these conversations have great psychological force for children. That is, whatever children do or do not bring to a conversation about the past, it is clear from many recent studies on children's references to the past that they are extremely interested in this kind of talk, that they pay special attention when others describe a past experience they participated in, and that they are often eager to try and relate their experiences. Reminiscing is, even for the youngest children, a gripping activity.

## How children's memories are influenced

As a spate of studies have now demonstrated, many parents refer to the personal past frequently, and do so in just such a way that is likely to engage their young partner's interest. The way they introduce talk about the past signals to the child that something special is going on ("Charlotte, remember when we fed the ducks? It was raining and our bread crumbs got all soggy. Remember that?"). They often tag their autobiographical references with "remember when" statements, letting their listener know what kind of thinking and interacting is about to happen. Many parents describe enough of a past episode to give the child a mental representation, a narrative, which she can envision and then augment. Research has shown that not all parents do this, nor do all cultures do it to the same extent or in the same situations. These individual and cultural variations notwithstanding, the process of engaging children in talk about the past is ubiquitous. And one clear way to make sure a child enters into the activity is to talk about the past in a way in which he or she can and wants to relate.

If adults have such a powerful influence on how young children recall specific events, and how more generally they construct autobiographical narratives, we might ask how this influence is reflected in cultural differences. A recent addition to the growing body of research on this topic has been a look at the ways in which cultures might vary regarding how they talk about the past with their youngest members. For instance, Mary Mullen has found that Korean mothers and their children refer to the past less frequently and are less likely to focus on the personal experience of a past event. Mullen argues that this is con-sonant with a culture that de-emphasizes the individual and instead focuses on the group experience. Jessica Han, Michelle Leichtman, and Qi Wang compared the autobiographical narratives of 4- to 6-year-olds from Korea, China, and the United States and found that while all children showed age differences, and all children were equivalent in their overall memory capacity, they differed in what they recalled from past episodes. In line with Mullen's results they also found that American children were more likely to include descriptive terms, to include more references to internal states, and evaluations, and mention themselves as opposed to others, more often.

These results aren't all that surprising in light of important work done by the psychologists Hazel Markus and Shinobu Kitiyama showing that concepts of the self vary across cultures. Specifically they claimed that in Eastern cultures people think of themselves more in relation to others, as part of a group, while those in Western cultures are more likely to focus on the individual. One natural but still fascinating implication of this, supported by the work described above, is that how children recall the past and how the adults around them encourage them to recall their own past reflect culturally constructed views of the self.

Finally, in some cultural groups at least, parents invite their children into the activity by asking questions or making spaces in the description so that the child can contribute. All of these techniques for engaging children in descriptions of the past reflect the parents' possibly unconscious motivation to involve their children in what is an essential form of making meaning and creating a self.

The motivation is not merely pedagogical ("I want my child to learn about his past, I want my child to know how to construct a story about the past, I want my child to know what we in this culture view as good autobiographical talk"). As with lovers, some of the motivation is simply the urge to be close.

The intense attachment most 3-year-olds feel toward their mother or father does indeed hold the seeds of most subsequent forms of passion. Much of the intimacy between parent and child grows out of the mere fact of dependence, or if one is lucky, the experience of being loved and nurtured. But parents also do things with their children that help establish and sustain a sense of unique and ongoing intimacy. One of these things is to share experiences. And key to the sharing of experiences is the process of recollecting.

Some of the data coming out of studies on parent-child talk about the past attests to the emotional force of shared remembering. Parents and children tend to talk about emotionally charged experiences. As

Peggy Miller has shown in her studies of families in Baltimore, children seem to plumb reminiscing for two levels of emotional action: a reliving of the feeling they had at the time of the sad or exciting event, and whatever emotions they elicit from their parents while telling about the experience.

As with lovers, toddlers and their parents often seem to remember collaboratively as an act of closeness. While no systematic research has been done yet, most of us collecting naturalistic data on early reminiscing can attest to the suspended activity, the look of rapt attention the toddler gives the parent as she begins to talk about something they did days ago. This sudden shift in attention suggests to some of us that at 16 to 18 months, children already know or are beginning to realize that there is something special or distinctive about remembering. But not only does that activity itself seem to captivate them, the interaction between the child and the collaborator (often a parent) seems particularly attuned. The best analogy that comes to mind is the way two trapeze artists watch each other. Talking about the past with a parent requires the same kind of close attention, almost absorption, to put together an account of the past.

As two people exchange memories, they influence one another's memories. Memories are transformed as they are listened to and shared. For the youngest rememberer, this shaping can seem quite apparent. The child refers to an experience from the past and looks to the parent to expand on that reference. How the parent does so will in turn have a formative effect on the child's final representation.

A little girl, Maya, has just turned 4. Several people have asked her what she did on her birthday. To each she has shrugged and said, in a nonchalant, dismissive manner, "Noth'n much." In each case her mother, Saskia, opens her mouth in surprise, looks disbelievingly at Maya and at the guest, and says, "Didn't you have a party? Tell Susan about your party." How she responds to this has varied, from nothing at all to a brief description of how Miranda and Malcolm came and they all went swimming. To no one has she volunteered information about her presents, her cake, the baseball game, or the point at which all three went down under a large maple tree and took off all their clothes. It is impossible to know why she is reticent. Perhaps the party didn't mean that much to her. Perhaps it was a grave disappointment and that is what she wants to convey. Perhaps she thinks it is suave of her to downplay it. Perhaps she just doesn't know how to tell about it. What is apparent is her mother's effort to get her to talk about it.

Saskia signals to Maya what she thinks was significant about her party. She signals that she thinks it is worthwhile to tell people about an event like that. And she signals, at some more subtle level, that she wants Maya to remember her birthday in a particular way. Saskia is doing what many parents in many communities do—subtly influencing, perhaps even instructing, her child in the value of certain kinds of recollection and how Maya will reconstruct this particular episode.

Take, on the other hand, a story Maya is delighted to repeat again and again to any friendly listener. Her story goes like this:

> You see this? You see this scratch? [She points to a long, ugly scratch on the back of her thigh and her bottom.] We were walking to the chicken house. And I said, something is in my pants. And Scottie didn't know there was anything there. So we kept walking. But there was a stick up my butt!

This small piece of autobiography will evaporate before long. Surely it's not destined for the long-term collection of memoirs that we each acquire. But in the short run it serves as a prototype of autobiographical exchange. She tells it as a way of drawing people into who she is and what she has lived. And, perhaps unwittingly, she reveals to the analytic ear what matters to her, what kind of self in the past she wants to portray and mull over. She can relive the drama of the moment and extract some drama from the present moment as well, by shocking the listener with her misfortune, by amusing the listener with the twist in the tale (something much worse had happened to her than she or her companion had believed at the time).

The influence on a story like this happens at a subtler level. No one urges her to tell the story or adds elements to make it the story he or she thinks it should be. But the listener's shock, amusement, or sympathy acts as influencing factors on the teller's autobiographical gestures, as we might call them.

## How friends influence each other's memories

Influencing memories is not the sole domain of parents. Young friends can exert a powerful influence on one another as they tell each other about things from their past. Take for example two 5-year-olds sitting at a snack table at their day care center. One points to a burn on the other's lip.

"How did it get burned?"
"At home."
"Did it hurt when you got it?"
Child nods.

This may seem like a meaningless, ephemeral snippet of conversation between two momentary friends. In fact, it is the foundation of a kind of exchange that follows most of us through life. We make contact with one another through our past lives, as well as through the actions we carry out in the present. One child reaches out to the other by showing interest not only in the burn, but in the history of the burn ("How did it get burned?"). The child answers by telling where she got it, not how. Each child has a decision to make at each turn about what to say and what not to say. Then the initiator of the episode does the most interesting piece of remembering work. He asks about how his friend experienced what happened ("Did it hurt?"). This points to the primacy of what Jerome Bruner has called the subjective nature of autobiographical thinking. What matters about most people's past is what they thought and felt. These feelings and thoughts center around events (a burn, a move to a new town, a baby brother, a marriage, a tornado), but at the crux of a memory are the feelings and thoughts that surround the action.

What the snippet of conversation above shows is that even 5-year-olds focus on the subjective nature of the past. And even more interesting, they do this through transaction. The subjective nature of the past emerges as people connect through their talk about the past. In another conversation between two 5-year-olds, the use of the past to establish alliance is quite straightforward. The following conversation took place while two children were drawing at a table at their day care center:

CHILD 1:    Remember the other day when we went to the frog pond?

CHILD 2:    Yeah.

CHILD 1:    I was the only one who saw the frog.

CHILD 2:    Not'n. I saw one too.

CHILD 1:    No you didn't.

CHILD 2:    Did too.

CHILD 1:    Okay, but only you and I did. No one else. Okay?

CHILD 2:    (grinning) Yeah!

Again, the past is used to make connection between people. And again, even 5-year-olds veer toward the subjective aspect of the event—what was seen, and by whom.

It is not only through direct suggestion and question asking that parents and peers influence one another's recollections. There are all sorts of contexts for remembering, and not only does each one direct the kind of remembering that is done, but also the people within the context influence one another. It is often the case that a particular kind of reminiscing is somewhat contagious. Everyone will recognize the image of a dinner table conversation among adults, in which one person tells a self-deprecating story about the past. It is highly likely that the next two or three stories told by others at the table will also be self-deprecating. To some extent, this is explained by what the sociologist Erving Goffman called "maintaining a line." The great illuminator of social interactions, Goffman argued that once a person has set up a certain "face" or persona others will collude to help that person maintain his persona, his story, his self-presentation. Once someone has put him- or herself out there in a certain light, the overwhelming tendency is for others to support that perspective or light rather than contradict it. But it is also the case that we help someone maintain his or her "line" by creating similar lines ourselves. Thus, one story of personal failure is likely to lead to another, one story of old love is likely to lead to a series of lost romances, and so on. Not only the topic but often the theme or tone is maintained and elaborated by each person's story. This kind of contagion manifests itself in all kinds of settings and at a variety of levels. Sometimes it is the tone of the reminiscences and sometimes it is the topic. Children are as susceptible as are any table of adults. A class of third-graders was given the task of writing memories. In one group 80 percent wrote about successes and failures in sports. In another class, when asked to write family stories, all students but one wrote stories about their grandparents. Children exert influence over one another's remembering in much the way a group of adult friends do.

## From mutuality to conflict

Children between the ages of 18 months and 3 years are extremely dependent on a conversational partner to construct and tell a memory. In the following example, a 2-year-old and his father discuss a recent accident. The two build the memory collaboratively.

CHILD:  I hit my toe.

FATHER:  Yeah, you picked up that big rock and dropped it right on your toe.

CHILD:   It bleeded.

FATHER:   Yes, it bled a lot and we had to go to the emergency room.

CHILD:   That man didn't have a nose.

FATHER:   That's right. There was a guy at the hospital without a nose. That scared you didn't it? That was kind of icky.

One might say that at this stage memory is an intersubjective activity. As I described earlier, research has shown that as children develop, usually between the ages of 2 1/2 and 4, they acquire strong enough narrative skills and a stable enough extended self to recall things without the input of another person, even to the point of disagreeing with someone about what did or didn't happen.

This emerging independence has huge ramifications for the experience and uses of autobiographical memory. For a *New York Times* article about Barry Sonnenfeld's memories of his childhood, the filmmaker and his mother, whom it seems he despises, were interviewed. The conflicts between what each says about Sonnenfeld's youth capture painfully well the extreme alternative to the mutuality of early reminiscing.

Gleefully neurotic, he [Sonnenfeld] talks about everything: his inner fears, his family life, the rigors of making movies in a world of egomaniacs and bean counters, the countless childhood wounds that he cannot help but pick open again and again.

"You want to know how overprotected I was?" he asked. "My mother, who was an art teacher at my elementary school, took me to eat lunch with the teachers every day. I didn't eat with the other children until I was in the sixth grade."

(His mother, in a later interview, remembered it differently: "He was very, very shy. He always had a lot of friends around the apartment, but outside the building, he didn't participate in social activities.")

"All I ate was TV dinners," Mr. Sonnenfeld said, "I'd have two every night. Turkey was the best. The fried shrimp was good, too. One of the happiest days of my life was when they came out with the Hungry Man line. Every now and then, my mother would decide to get exotic and make egg salad. Do you know what happens if you leave eggs boiling too long on the stove? The water boils away, the pot scorches, the eggs get hotter and hotter and, eventually, they launch. I can remember coming into the apartment and there was this horrible smell and eggs all over the ceiling."

("He was a terrible eater and a fussy eater," Mrs. Sonnenfeld said. "He ate the same things over and over again, night after night. The only thing he loved, besides those TV dinners, was lamb chops."

Mr. Sonnenfeld remembers a couple of lamb chop grease fires, too.

The real, crystallizing moment, though, came during the night of April 22, 1970. "I remember the date. It was the first Earth Day, and I was at the concert with my girlfriend. It was something like 2 in the morning and Jimi Hendrix was tuning up, and suddenly over the loudspeaker system came the words 'Barry Sonnenfeld, please call your mother.'"

("That's his version," Mrs. Sonnenfeld said. "There are always two versions, the parents' version and the kid's version. I think he had a wonderful childhood, and he was the easiest kid in the world to grow up with.")

The article is a marvelous if unwitting demonstration of how people negotiate a shared past. Here two people, not just any two people but an aging mother and her adult son, reminisce to a third party about the same events. The son obviously sees the memories he is sharing as crystallizations of his whole childhood. And clearly he sees these memories as the base of his current self. They are explanatory memories. But there is also a current, transactional force to them. And this force is multilayered. His quotes are public in more ways than one. They are directed at an interviewer but with an eye toward a larger audience. And they are directed toward a smaller and more specific, tangible audience as well, his mother. The memories converge in that the point of contention is the same in each quote—Sonnenfeld's sociability, his eating habits, and the intensity of the bond between mother and son. In fact, they agree about the events as well. She doesn't contradict his claim that he didn't sit with other children. She doesn't contradict his basic claim about what he ate. And she doesn't contradict what happened on Earth Day.

But her view of these events and what they signify is completely different from his. The overall meaning of those events and what they may or may not illuminate or explain about his current life is totally different for the two rememberers. This is an example at odds with Goffman's generative description of how people support one another's self-presentation. This is a case in which two people, for complex and emotionally charged reasons, use the past to shake up one another's self-presentations. In any collaborative effort there is potential for cooperation and for conflict. When people build the past together, their disagreements are as constitutive of the past as are their collusions.

## What remembering does for friends

Recently I went to a friend's house to say hello to her son, who was visiting from out of town. I know the young man and his two buddies who were there, in a casual way. They sat around talking while I sat listening. They didn't discuss anything. In fact, there were almost no questions and answers, propositions or rebuttals, or even jointly told stories. Instead, in a somewhat laconic manner, they took turns telling stories about experiences they had shared in the past. At some point one of them looked through the window at a neighbor's house, turned back to his friends, and all three more or less simultaneously said, in an exaggerated way, "Geet up the hill, puppy, geet up the hill." They were referring to a funny episode from their shared past in which one of them, John, had gone to speak to the neighbor, whose huge, vicious dog had leapt out at him. The neighbor, an obese and toothless woman, had called out laconically to the dog, "Geet up the hill puppy," and when the dog continued to launch himself toward John, had reached her arm out of the screen door, grabbed the dog by the collar, and hauled him inside. This story gets repeated every time these three friends are together. It holds all kinds of humor and reference points for them. And now, after all these years, all it takes is for one of them to glance at the neighbor's house, and all three evoke the whole story, with the key phrase, "Geet up the hill, puppy."

I was startled by the seeming lack of interchange. Then I realized that they were doing the most natural thing in the world: they were reconnecting after a long separation by remembering past shared experiences. There are two ways friends use the past in the service of friendship. One is to exchange experiences as a way of becoming close, getting to know one another. Typically, when people first become friends they are eager, like Lara and Yuri in Pasternak's *Dr. Zhivago,* to tell one another about who they are, where they come from, what they have experienced. The experiences they exchange are not random, or complete. They tell those stories that explain or convey the person they are—"I am what I have lived." As people continue a friendship they are very likely to spend some of their time retelling shared experiences. This is most common among friends who don't get to spend a lot of time together. Going over and over the same stories is a way of re-establishing connection, by re-establishing the past. For very good friends who have done this a lot, the past becomes coded with short phrases that stand for long stories.

The anthropologist Brad Shore remembers what was for him a pivotal experience while doing fieldwork in Samoa in the 1970s. Upon returning to his household one day from his regular run, he found the village in an uproar. Tuato, the village chief, had been murdered. Shore describes the aftermath of the murder, particularly the ways in which people retold and explained what had happened. The villagers used remembering not only as a way of making sense of what had happened, but also as a way of participating in what had happened as well:

> All over the village, people were doing their own recollecting, recounting their stories, again and again, compulsively telling what they had seen or heard, where they had been when the shot rang out, how the man with the rifle had locked himself in his father's house. Gradually, from out of these stories would come a "line" — the seed of some kind of coherent "take" on the murder. In some cases, it was the drink that figured in the story, alcohol which everyone knew brought out the devil in people. Other accounts stressed old histories of conflict between men.

In other words, telling and trading stories about what happened became the sequel to what happened. While the comparing and melding of stories helped the community come to some shared sense of the event, it also allowed people to participate, if only through the activity of recollection, in the drama itself. Shore also points out that these personal recollections of a publicly significant event capture perfectly the intersection of the internal and the external aspects of human experience.

> The stories were all personal fictions, made on the fly, but they were neither entirely personal nor completely fictional. Such story telling necessarily exploits a limited range of conventional narrative models, even as it is experienced as a free wheeling account of what "really" happened.

As people recount experiences to one another they identify and communicate what is idiosyncratic and private. At the same time, they exchange and build on shared versions of what has happened. Shore's extended example demonstrates the way in which it is the comparing, contrasting, and blending of versions of an episode that both reflects the culture's structure and values and serves to strengthen, change, or extend that structure and those values.

Shore's discussion of personal recounting also shows that people use the past as a way to explain things. The villagers construct stories about what happened that will make one moment, one act—the murder—comprehensible. The sentence "Tuato was murdered" would merely refer to something in the past. But it requires a story (or many stories) that lead up to that important moment to create either an individual or a shared form of autobiographical memory. In creating such stories the members of Shore's host village constructed their own explanations for what happened and why.

Interestingly, there is a second layer to this idea: Shore himself is using the story of a past event to explain something—the story of the murder and its aftermath demonstrates the ways in which people's minds are shaped by their culture. In other words people use the past to explain themselves, their ideas, and their cultures. In this particular case the participants in the murder, members of the victim's community, and an anthropologist all use the event for different purposes. It brings to mind the philosopher Paul Ricouer's statement, "This is the time to remind ourselves that in most European languages, the term 'history' has an intriguing ambiguity, meaning both what really happens and the narrative of those events." (In Chapter 6 I'll develop this idea, that an event and its retellings comprise many layers of what we think of as history.)

Throughout this discussion I have been talking about the ways in which situations define the process of memory. One important dimension of situations in which two people remember together concerns whether they are recalling an experience in which they both participated or are exchanging recollections that are new or unknown to the other. The ramifications of each are central to the context of the memory, since people recall shared experiences as a way of confirming their intimacy, of finding common ground, and of reigniting the feelings they had at that earlier moment. Of course, it's a whole other ball game if the people involved remember it differently. Barry Sonnenfeld and his mother recall the past in sharply contrasting ways, though they don't recall the basic elements differently. It is not uncommon, however, for members of a family or partners in a marriage to recall the basic facts of the past very differently. This phenomenon is a particularly pungent experience. Most of us can evoke the experience of describing something that has happened only to have someone else in the room insist that it didn't happen at all, or that it happened in an altogether different way. The experience of hearing that feels almost like an assault. This is remarkable given that many of us readily acknowledge that memory is a constructive process, and that it is the rule rather than the exception to create idiosyncratic subjective descriptions of the past.

Whenever I teach a college course about memory, I ask the students whether they have ever gone back home during a school vacation and found themselves in a violent disagreement with a sibling over some event from childhood. And the question never fails to elicit slightly surprised looks of acknowledgment, as if to say, "How did she know my sister and I had a bitter fight over who got punished when the house caught fire?" For all that we know about the subjective and constructive nature of memory, it is still a shock to find that someone else remembers it differently. The strength of our emotional reaction when our version of the past is challenged is an indication of how attached we become to our recollections, and how powerful is the urge to have control over one's own past.

## Mechanisms of distortion

When people recall the past together, one of the most volatile dimensions of the experience concerns the kind and amount of distortion that occur. Recalling a shared experience is one thing when you agree completely or accept the other person's description. It is another experience altogether to find yourself reminiscing about what seems to be a wholly different event than the one your friend recalls. It is likely that if you and, say, a sibling differ about an event from long ago, you will assume it is your sibling who has forgotten, distorted, or is lying. It is much harder to examine one's own processes of forgetting and distortion than to think the other person's memory is fallible. (I am referring here to unintended distortions where the rememberer absolutely believes what he is recalling. Deliberate lying is another matter.)

It is a jarring experience to confront this kind of discrepancy, though just how jarring depends on why you are reminiscing in the first place, what the reverberations and consequences are of disagreement, and who you are disagreeing with and about what kind of experience. Thanks to a great deal of research in this area, we now understand some of the mechanisms that cause us to distort, which in turn helps us predict situations and individuals who will be most susceptible to certain kinds of distortion.

## Self as center of the past

We all tend to put ourselves at the center of the past. Why else create one? Why else remember? Even when we recall events that had ramifications for others, events in which we played a small part, we tend to magnify our own role and shift things so that they more directly relate to us. The social psychologist Anthony Greenwald has referred to this as the totalitarian ego. The self tends to appear more central, more important, and have more of an impact than what "really happened." If five people were involved in an event, each will tell of that event so that he or she, the teller, appears as the central character.

While Greenwald talks about this in purely psychological terms, one can also think of it in literary terms. Every story has both a narrator and a central character, someone through whose eyes the story unfolds. We all put ourselves in the center of action. This coincides nicely with the argument made by some that to remember is to tell a story, and all stories must have a hero. Clearly, one is always the narrator of one's memory. But what is fascinating is that we also tend to make ourselves the hero of the past. It is rare for someone to tell a story about his or her own experience and make someone else in the story more important. In novels, the narrator can take a variety of perspectives on the hero. Jane Austen views her heroine Emma with love and irony. Even so, Emma remains central to all that happens in the same way that we recall ourselves as the pivotal person in any recollection. We are both narrator and hero of our own past.

One of the theories that has most to say about how and why we distort the past is the theory of cognitive dissonance. Leon Festinger's groundbreaking work stated that whenever a person holds two thoughts that are in conflict, or a thought and an action that are in conflict, he or she will experience dissonance, or discomfort, and will be motivated to change one of those thoughts to reduce the dissonance. For instance, if I think of myself as a nurturing, supportive mother, and then I harshly criticize my son, I am likely to experience dissonance. How can that behavior be consonant with my self-image? When faced with that kind of dissonance I have several choices. I can accept that I am not the nurturing mother I thought I was, or I can figure out an explanation that causes the two things to be less dissonant (the criticism was actually good for him and, therefore, ultimately nurturing, I was under special duress that made it an exception to my usual personality, and so on). Elliot Aronson modified and added to Festinger's original formulation by arguing that we are most vulnerable to dissonance when it involves our self-concept. Further, he has argued, we all want to believe that we are both consistent and good. Therefore, when our behavior challenges our self-image as a consistent and good person, we are most likely to experience dissonance and be motivated to reduce that dissonance by changing one of our cognitions or constructing an explanation that makes our cognitions and behaviors less dissonant.

We use the process of memory to reduce dissonance. If we are always working to maintain a positive and consistent self-concept, then one of the main ways we can do this is through the stories we tell about what has happened. For instance, having harshly criticized my son, all I have at my disposal to reduce any dissonance I feel is to recall the episode in a way that makes me less harsh or explains the harsh criticism in a way that is consonant with my self-image as nurturing and gentle. Recollections of the immediate and distant past allow us to reduce dissonance and maintain a positive self-concept. In one of the most brilliant depictions of dissonance reduction at work, George Eliot describes the plight of her haunting hero, Tertius Lydgate, in *Middlemarch*. Lydgate, the ambitious and idealistic young doctor, must vote for one of two men to become chaplain of the new infirmary. Lydgate believes Farebrother to be the better of the two men, but Lydgate's benefactor wants another man, Tyke, to win. Lydgate ends up choosing Tyke, thereby ensuring his own good standing with his benefactor. At first the thought of his own self-interest guiding his vote makes him terribly uneasy. Over time he comes to see that in fact he chose the better man. He initially thinks of Farebrother this way, "But his liking for the Vicar of St. Botolph's grew with growing acquaintanceship . . . [he] showed an unusual delicacy and generosity which Lydgate's nature was keenly alive to." Gradually Lydgate rewrites events such that his vote represents the wise rather than self-interested choice. By the end of the chapter his views about Farebrother (against whom he voted) have changed: "Lydgate thought that there was a pitiable infirmity of will in Mr. Farebrother."

How does this help us in reinterpreting the distortions of memory? Well, you can bet that if people recall an episode from the past, there are two kinds of distortions they are likely to make based on dissonance theory: they are likely to make themselves out to be better than they are, and they are likely to make themselves out to be more consistent than they are.

There are some interesting wrinkles to this claim. For one thing, some researchers have been surprised to find that when they recall episodes from their past, they do in fact recall as many negative episodes as positive ones. In one study, Willem Wagenaar kept a diary of daily events for a period of 12 months. At the end of the year he used different kinds of cues (who, what, where, and when) to recall various episodes that had been recorded. To his surprise he remembered as many negative as positive events. What does this mean in light of what has been said about the need to see oneself in a positive light? Wagenaar suggests that we recall these negative events as a way of explaining them, highlighting them in contrast to our *usually* positive deeds and behavior. In that sense none of us are simplistic rememberers. We are all smart enough to know that we must have done some bad things, but that they are notable because they are so unusual and can be used to point out how good we are most of the time.

As mentioned earlier, one way in which the ego dominates memory is by making our role bigger and more important in an event than others experienced it to be. For instance, take any committee or group of people working on a project together. It is common for each person, when interviewed separately, to describe his or her own role in positive changes as a central one. Politicians regularly take credit for productive changes in legislation, even when in reality they only played a small part in a complex group process. All of us do the same thing, though less deliberately and with less obvious ulterior motives. Without any gross differences in what might be called facts, the way the story is constructed shifts one's role in it. And to Anthony Greenwald's point, the teller of the story is likely to exaggerate his role in the main event. A striking and somewhat poignant example of this occurs when young children recall a family catastrophe and cite themselves as the cause of the problem. One mother tells the story of the family dog slicing its foot on a can top in the field. Three years later, while reminiscing, her 7-year-old son insists that the dog cut its foot because he left his pocket knife lying on the kitchen floor. Two separate events had been merged and had put him as the cause of the accident. While in this case guilt rather than self-aggrandisement explains the distortion, in both cases the self is central to the story.

In her book *Positive Illusions,* Shelley Taylor says that we often use this mechanism to support and preserve our well-being. Taylor claims that there are a host of ways in which we deceive ourselves to make life seem better. She considers these illusions to be healthy and adaptive and a normal part of most people's everyday life. In fact, she points out that people who are more realistic than the average are also more depressed. Among the common self-deceptions that she describes are several that bear on memory. For instance, research shows that most of us overestimate our ability to achieve a goal: jump a certain distance, win a game, score high on a test, get a particular job. Taylor claims that our overestimation helps motivate us and increases our chances of succeeding. We attempt things we might never try if we realistically faced our low chance of succeeding. In another body of research, groups of people are put to work together on a task. After the task, participants were asked individually how much of a contribution they made. Everyone overestimated his or her own contribution to the activity, and the contribution percentages consistently added up to much more than 100 percent. If Taylor is correct, then distortion is a regulating mechanism that helps us get through the day. Reality is not what we should deal with; in fact, what makes us human is our ability to make reality seem better than it really is. One part of the reality we positively distort is ourselves.

Cognitive dissonance theory tells us that people want to think of themselves as consistent. And they will distort things that make them appear inconsistent. Research has shown that in fact this directly affects our recollection of previously held attitudes. George Goethals and Richard Reckman did a study almost 20 years ago in which they had students state an opinion on a controversial topic, for example, busing. Then those students participated in a seminar in which they were led to change their minds. At the end of the seminar they were asked to recall their opinion at the beginning of the semester. A great majority of them misremembered their former opinion when that opinion differed from their current one. We like to see ourselves as consistent, and in the face of a powerful new idea or belief it is easier to change the past than explain the change or give up on the new belief.

To see firsthand how this works, and just how powerful it can be, try the following thought experiment. Ask some people whose political views have changed dramatically over the past 10 years who they voted for 10 years ago and who they voted for in the most recent election. Then ask them to explain the vote they made 10 years ago. Chances are they will change the story of their old politics to make a cohesive line between then and now. The social psychologists Michael Ross and Michael Conway performed just this experiment, comparing people's present positions on certain topics to their opinions or situations 10 years earlier. Ross and Conway found that people have implicit theories of personal development and that they reshape the story of their past to fit their idea of how they should have developed. If they have changed their views or situations, they are likely to recast their old views to make their implicit theory of personal development coherent. Distorting old views to make them consistent with current views makes people feel stable and predictable. Do all our personal memories fall prey to this impulse?

What kinds of interactions lead people to change their memories? In the example of voting, one is motivated by a need for internal consistency. But this kind of dissonance reduction is also at work between people. People influence one another in their versions of the past. Will Mrs. Sonnenfeld cement her view of things, or will she change it to assimilate what Barry says? Do the people in Samoa modulate their stories of the murder to incorporate what they hear in one another's stories?

In fact, the influence of others on one's memory is startlingly powerful. People can be led by others to remember what they have not really experienced. Some circumstances are more likely than others to make you responsive to suggestion. Saul Kassin and his colleagues set up an experiment in which college students were given a computer task and told under no circumstances should they press a certain key. At some point the experimenter rushed in, announcing that the key had been pressed and a great deal of valuable data had been lost. The participant was then told to go. Upon leaving the lab, another college student (a confederate in the study) came up to the participant and asked what had happened in the lab. In a majority of the cases the participants told the student in the hallway that they had inadvertently pressed the forbidden key. In a number of cases, the subject went on to recall specific aspects of the momentary accident. In fact, no key had been pushed, but the subject had been led to recall something that had never happened. Kassin's setup is one where you would be likely to accept the input of the imposing interlocutor. On the other hand, when arguing with an adversary (in a divorce or in a business meeting, for example) differences between versions are likely to make you dig in your heels and become even more adamant about your view of what happened.

The writer Lawrence Wright documented the now famous case in which a member of a Washington State police department, Paul Ingram, was accused by his children of satanic ritual abuse. What made the case even more grimly fascinating than the basic charges was that while at first Ingram insisted he was innocent, during the investigation period he came to confess that he had, in fact, committed sustained abuse against his children. His confession was so deeply felt, and so clearly communicated, that he described many of the occurrences of abuse in some detail. The social psychologist Richard Ofshe was brought in during the investigation to help figure out what was going on. At one point Ofshe asked Ingram to talk about an incident that in actuality was made up by Ofshe. At first Ingram said he couldn't remember it. Then he said he needed to go pray (the townsfolk, members of the police department, and Ingram's family in particular were deeply committed to their fundamentalist beliefs). He returned from praying to say he did recall the act of abuse to which Ofshe was referring, and proceeded to elaborate on the brief information Ofshe had given. Finally, it was shown that in fact these confessions were not based on reality, that in fact Ingram had *not* committed acts of abuse against his children.

This case is a dramatic demonstration of the ways in which our memories are vulnerable to suggestion. Ingram was led to believe he had committed atrocious acts that in fact he had not committed. Suggestion alone is probably not enough to cause someone to suffer this dramatic a case of memory distortion. At play no doubt are various personality characteristics of Paul Ingram. In addition, a case could be made for the idea that living in such a restrictive community (both the police force and the church imposing stringent constraints on individual experience) led to a level of repression of fantasy such that, under the bizarre circumstances, his long-repressed fantasies provided material for his false memories. In other words, while his confessions did not accurately represent his past deeds, in some sense they may have represented fantasies that were deeply repressed because of his religious beliefs, social environment, and the nature of his work experience. If this construction is true, it suggests that someone who persistently represses unconscious material, who structures an overly rigid and oppressive set of rules to live and think by, may be more subject to certain kinds of distortion than other people. While past events may not have been repressed by Ingram, it is possible that past fantasies were, and that in the context of his daughters' accusations, and the censure of his community, these fantasies were confused with memories.

In more everyday circumstances, the ways in which we influence one another's memories are probably not so dramatic, nor so pernicious. Nonetheless, we are all vulnerable to the deliberate and unconscious impact that other people's memories and responses have on our own representations of what has happened in the past.

What people expect from a memory, or from the rememberer, also influences the transaction. If you expect people to be accurate about events, you will listen and respond differently than if you assume that distortion is the rule. In some cases your estimation of accuracy comes from the role a person is fulfilling (a teacher is likely to expect a co-teacher to be more accurate in recalling an incident than a child would be, a therapist to be more accurate than his or her patient, and so on). On the other hand, in some cases it is one's judgment about a particular person that dictates expectations of accuracy. You are likely to hear the memories of a friend who often lies differently than you are the memories of someone known for his or her meticulous accounts. Furthermore, if you believe that memory is a function of biological processes and is determined internally rather than socially, you will no doubt expect a level of consistency that might not be realistic.

The psychologists Lee Ross and Richard Nisbett have shown that in our culture people are likely to explain behavior by internal attributes, while Chinese people attribute behavior to the situation. Thus, in our culture we believe that a person's remembering expresses a core self rather than meeting the demands of the current situation. If two people meet in a business context and disagree on what happened at the previous meeting, they can do one of two things: battle it out until one person's version of events is accepted by everyone, or accept the difference and move on. However, people who are likely to have a long-term relationship may anticipate many situations in which they will need to discuss the past. For intimates, or prospective intimates, disagreement about the past can be a source of terrible strife. What we expect from a stranger in negotiating the past is quite different from what we expect from a close friend or relative. In addition, we all carry around with us internal models of memory. As Ross and Nisbett's work shows, in our culture we are likely to think that what people recall is a function of what they actually experienced, coupled with what we see as idiosyncracies in their personality that make them distort in one way or another. On the other hand, people who are brought up in Asian cultures are more likely to understand that the situation in which one does the recalling exerts a large influence on what is recalled. Each time we engage in a discussion about the past with another person, our implicit ideas about how memory works shape what we hear and what we do with what we hear.

The research described in this chapter shows that mechanisms of distortion are powerful, pervasive, and in many ways, adaptive. It should not be surprising then that people so often disagree about what has happened in the past. What makes memory exchanges particularly volatile is that while subjectivity and distortion are the rule, agreeing on the past seems to be essential to our sense of intimacy, well-being, and personal cohesion. And while distortion is the rule, the amazing and important fact is that much of the time our memories are accurate enough that we find general agreement with others about most of what has happened in the course of daily life. For most mentally well people, memories are constrained by reality and conform to a large degree to an objective and consensual version of events.

Given the range of dynamics that can come into play when two people recall the past, it should be easy to see that there is no single process, internal or external, that can account for remembering. Thus far I have discussed developmental characteristics, the role of language and narrative, and the kind of social interaction and cultural forces that influence exchanges of autobiographical memory. But the more tangible external characteristics of a situation also have an impact on how and what people remember. Both the time and the structure of a setting shape the process and substance of what people recall about their lives. The kind of remembering two or more people create in conversation can happen in a minute, an hour, or across years of friendship and familiarity. These different time frames in which people collaborate or clash in recalling the past affect what one expects or takes from the remembering situation. And not all memory exchanges emerge casually within the flow of relationships and daily communications. In most cultures, certainly in ours, there are also more well-defined and public settings in which people create the past in response to one another.

# CHAPTER THREE

# COURTROOMS AND THERAPY ROOMS

One's memory never stands alone. Or, to be more precise, one never remembers outside of some context, some situation that shapes the thing we know as remembering. The settings in which one remembers, and thus what it means to remember, vary dramatically. For instance, think of the unbidden memory that comes to mind while walking to work one morning. The smell that drifts out from a store triggers a long-buried image from childhood. As you wander alone down the street, between one social group—your family—and another—your colleagues—a deeply personal, perhaps never before experienced, much less articulated, recollection has surfaced. Depending on the significance of the memory, your mood and state of mind, and your temperament (tendency to dwell on personal reflection, tendency to disregard internal experiences), you will save the thought, share it at work, muse over it, incorporate it into your day (as an anecdote, as a fragment of the article you are writing, as a source of personal insight, as something to share with your children when you get home). Or you may slip right over it, sending it back to the seemingly unstructured, often unreachable land of your unconscious.

Now contrast this with a courtroom in which you are appearing as a witness in a trial. You have been called to the stand to recall an accident you happened to see several weeks before. You arrive at the court already thinking of yourself as someone with an important memory. You know that others know you are there to describe a memory, and you may know something of what others recall or think about the incident. Perhaps you know that others have said that one of the cars was swerving, even though you have been asked to testify because you recall that car as moving slowly and steadily. You will certainly have rehearsed, possibly with the help of an attorney, what you recall, going over exactly what you will and won't say. It may be that the incident you recall has no personal reverberations or connotations save its status in making you a witness in a court case.

What could be more different than these two situations, the reasons behind the remembering and the expectations you and others have about your memory? (As we saw Chapters 1 and 2, one of the most important determinants of the memory process is whether you are alone or with others when you recall something from the past.) Another hugely important feature is how formal the setting is and how salient the process of remembering is within that setting. In our culture, we have created certain highly articulated contexts for remembering, well-defined contexts that have important consequences for communal life. In these settings we have unspoken but no less powerfully defined ideas about what memory is and for what it should be used. These contexts also often contain their own rules or features that shape how memories are constructed and exchanged.

Two such settings in modern life are the courtroom and the therapist's office. Though there are others, these two have come to play increasingly important roles in our social system, with legal, financial, as well as familial ramifications. Both settings have generated models and metaphors that shape our thinking in other contexts as well. The idea that it can be liberating to find out what childhood events explain one's current behavior is now a commonplace notion, extending far beyond the walls of the therapist's office.

To some extent the two systems, court and therapy, have come to support one another, often converging in the lives of an individual or a group (for instance, in child custody cases, sexual harassment cases, some murder cases). Memory invokes one set of rules and expectations in court and quite another in therapy. At times the rules and expectations in court contradict those at play in therapy. In other ways the two settings highlight some of the structural features of all remembering.

Imagine first the courtroom as a setting for recalling a memory. It's a place in which descriptions of the past are supposed to yield facts:

what really happened, who did and said what, and who was at fault. All dialogues between people include, by definition, specific roles for people to play. Spoken memories rest on a conversational structure, whether it be an actual dialogue between two or more people or the imagined interplay involved in writing or monologue. In other words, spoken memories involve roles (speakers and listeners, those who participated in a remembered event versus those who are hearing about it for the first time). The courtroom presents a somewhat unusual structuring of those roles in that there is a designated set of silent listeners. They cannot ask questions, but must listen and then make a final construction of an event based on all the things other people say about that event. There are also the designated question askers — the lawyers. Their task is to draw people out and get them to describe an event. But lawyers are not impartial, nor are they naive, or even open-minded questioners. They are strongly motivated to elicit a construction of the past that will fortify their claims and help them to win a case. They want the past to look a certain way in order to make the listeners (the jury) come up with a particular view of what happened.

Then there are the rememberers — the witnesses. These are individuals asked or directed to appear in front of a room full of people to describe something they have seen or in which they have participated. It is an intriguing setup. The witness's reliability is everything. Nuance is useless, or worse, distorting. A witness often has to answer all sorts of questions, hostile and rehearsed. Questions from the lawyer who asked them to testify will be rehearsed and leading; questions from the opposing side will be aggressive, aimed at creating doubt about the witness's ability to recall the scene accurately. In both cases, the kind of memory work demanded of the witness is highly constrained. In more casual circumstances, say, between friends, conversations ramble. A memory, or the act of remembering, may just emerge unplanned as some offshoot of another conversation. In the courtroom, however, the past is often the explicit and formally defined topic, with socially defined and concrete ramifications — losing or winning, guilt or innocence, jail or freedom.

The delineation of roles in the courtroom can make the act of constructing a memory a tricky one. For instance, a lawyer is out to create an impression of the past with a set of jurors. While he will shape the description through his questions, it is the witnesses who supposedly "have" the memories. And because it is in court and not in a living room, the lawyer has to guess how it will play to the jury, without any of the kind of collaborative listening described in Chapter 2.

A young public defender, Jenny, describes the unpredictable challenge of figuring out what narrative the jury is constructing based on what they hear from witnesses. She says,

> You never know what detail is going to hang them up — which thing they hear or don't hear is going to make your client's story seem implausible. I defended a guy, sort of down and out, practically homeless, who was being tried for petty theft. They claim he took some allergy medicine from the drugstore. He said he was wandering around, and the guy working in the store was watching him suspiciously. That made him angry. So he picked up the allergy medicine just to provoke the guy. He didn't plan to take it. Here is where his story broke down for the jury. When he was arrested he had some allergy medicine in his pocket. He insisted that he had brought that with him when he came into the store. But that he was looking to buy another kind that would work better. The jury, as it turned out later, just couldn't accept the idea that a man who already had some allergy medicine would want to buy more. I had no idea that was going to be the hole in the story that hung him. You just never know which thing is going to ruin the story for them.

In Sidney Lumet's classic film, *Twelve Angry Men,* we watch a group of jurors try to make sense of court testimony, as well as their reactions to that testimony. A key witness has claimed she could see the crime through her bedroom window, at some distance away. Later, while deliberating, one of the jurors realizes that the witness has indentation marks on her nose, showing that she normally wears glasses. How, then, could she have seen the crime while in bed? Suddenly, her testimony is in doubt and the whole story becomes suspect. The particular structure and sequence of the courtroom events make impossible the kind of repairs, explanations, and elaborations that regularly occur when people tell each other about the past.

What is special about the courtroom as a setting for memory is that unlike a normal conversation, in which the listener would communicate where he or she saw gaps, would ask probing questions, and in that way help the speaker construct a better story about the past, in the courtroom, the whole idea is not to let someone know where his or her account is flawed. A witness is supposed to construct a scene from the past without any feedback from the audience.

Picture the process a witness might go through in retrieving a memory on the stand. Very often, the witness has rehearsed the memory several times, with and without the input of others. There are two ways in which the witness might begin retrieving and rehearsing the memory. First, she knows she was present at a significant event. Ulric Neisser and others have shown that when you know an event is socially significant, you are likely to recall it differently than other more insignificant or private events. The implication is that when we encode memories, part of what we take in is our estimation of how other people view these events. William James said that we have as many selves as there are people who think about us. We can extend that reverberating thought and say that every memory is highlighted, distorted, and stored in terms of how we think others will think about it. A famous instance of this phenomenon, documented by Neisser, is the way in which people recall hearing that JFK had been assassinated. Most people remember where they were and what they were doing. But the public nature of the event shapes their construction of the memory. People's knowledge that this event matters to others influences the fact that they retrieve it and rehearse it.

A second more obvious trigger for retrieval and rehearsal would occur if you are subpoenaed and told you will be called as a witness regarding some event. In this case as well, you are directly or indirectly made aware of the public significance of your private experience of an event. This in itself is important. A deliberate search for an event already tagged as socially significant is going to be influenced by your sense of why the event is significant and what it means to others. You are likely to focus on the details you think others think are important. Often what one remembers of a less significant, more personal event is highly idiosyncratic. You might remember, as Virginia Woolf did, the pattern of flowers on someone's dress, yet not remember some element of the event that others deemed highly important. Or you might recall a detail that seems odd and meaningless, only to discover years later that the detail symbolizes some powerful and salient meaning of the event. The personal memory recalled alone can focus on any aspect of an event. On the other hand, if you are recalling an event because others have asked you to, or because you know it was an event with public significance, your attention will be directed to those aspects that make it significant (or that you suppose make it significant).

As noted in Chapter 2, research has shown that we tend to recall events in a way that confirms our current hypotheses about things. We all know how this works in informal everyday circumstances. For instance, imagine a child trying to convince her parent that a teacher is mean and that the punishment she received at school was unfair. If that child is asked to describe what happened in school, she is more than likely to reconstruct the event in a way that confirms her innocence and highlights the unpleasant and unreasonable nature of the teacher. Depending on your view of the overall situation, you are likely to look for evidence (in your memory) to confirm your working hypothesis about what happened. If you perceive your spouse as an angry and domineering person, you are likely to recall the last 10 years of marriage with a preponderance of events that emphasize your spouse's bossiness. You are less likely to recall, or recall vividly, those occasions on which his behavior contradicted your current view. In both these instances some of the work we do to make the past seem consonant with the present is in response to the attention of another person, whether that attention be skeptical or believing of what we say about the past. This is probably even more powerful in a highly organized formal setting such as a courtroom. If you come to court as a witness for the defense and have any reason to want to support the defendant, you are likely to recall the past in a way that confirms, overall, the innocence of the defendant. What is important to recognize in this setting is that this kind of distortion is the norm. One doesn't have to be evil or a liar to change the past in a way that confirms one's current beliefs. Many researchers now describe memory as a process by which we support the present.

In groundbreaking work performed more than 20 years ago, the developmental psychologist Ann Brown came up with the idea of meta-memory. In essence, her argument is that one of the most significant developmental shifts that occurs in the domain of memory concerns the level of awareness and deliberateness one has about how to remember. She showed that in addition to sheer memory span increasing as a function of maturation, children become aware that remembering is a specific task and that specific acts can improve memory (chunking things, using mnemonic devices, rehearsing, and so on.) This work is highly relevant to the idea presented here, that the deliberate and self-conscious nature of the witness's remembering task affects how he goes about recalling the past. In other words, the work we do to make the past lead up to the present shifts as a function of the attention we pay to the memory process itself.

Part of what distinguishes memory in a courtroom is the self-description, or role you take on in that setting. Much of the time in everyday life memory is a transparent or invisible process. You don't think about the fact that you are remembering but rather use memory in the service of whatever else you are doing (trying to convince someone to do what you want, merely passing the time with a friend, doing work that requires you to draw on past experiences, and so on). On the other hand, when you are called to the witness stand, your function is to recall something. This self-awareness about the process may in fact influence, or even constrain, the kind of remembering in which you engage.

One source of constraint comes from the fact that there may be a lot riding on what you recall. Possibly, it will affect the lives of others. The consequences of remembering in a courtroom setting are extremely important. Knowing that something rides on your memory changes how you monitor the process. Often our memories of the past seem to matter to no one but ourselves. Moreover, no one ever has the chance to question or verify our version of events. Think of all the snippets of childhood memories that float in and out of our consciousness, never making their way to a forum in which someone could challenge their veracity. And though our false memories may guide our actions and fuel our unhealthy behaviors, we are rarely aware that this is happening. The consequences of those private memories are rarely salient as such. Even in the negotiations of the past described in Chapter 2, the kinds that occur between friends or family members, disagreement leads to unpleasant feelings, a fight perhaps, or possibly even a revision of one's memory of a particular event. Rarely are the consequences of exchanging or changing memories between friends laid out ahead of time, nor are they ever ironclad. You could disagree with your brother about an event that took place 20 years ago, fight about it, go home and think more about the event, and change your mind. On the other hand, if you are recalling the past in a court of law, the consequences of your memory are quite salient. Your ability to remember will be under public scrutiny. You may hear others (the other witnesses) describe the same situation from different perspectives. Two lawyers with opposing motivations will ask you questions. So there will be a great deal of pressure on you to remember in a certain way. One lawyer may be trying to prove that your memory is reliable; the other may be trying to prove that your memory is unreliable.

Whatever pure image or scene you might have started with as a memory of the event is transformed forever by the context in which you use that memory. Imagine for a moment that you have a personal, perhaps unbidden recollection of a scene. Imagine that it turns out you are asked to testify about that scene. Now imagine the court session is over. The original unbidden memory is probably totally unavailable to you. It may not even exist anymore. The original internal image or scene, transformed through the process of communication and transaction, will become the internal memory, replacing the original private one.

A notorious example of this is the woman described by Lenore Terr in her book *Unchained Memories*. The woman, Eileen Franklin-Lipsker, testified in court that she was bathing her young daughter one day when something about the tilt of her daughter's head and the look on her face triggered a memory from 30 years ago. This unbidden image from the past precipitated a seemingly long buried memory of the rape and murder of Eileen's 10-year-old friend by Franklin-Lipsker's father, George Franklin. Her memory led her to therapy, during which she expanded on that unbidden moment and developed a full-fledged autobiographical narrative about what had happened all those years before. Her therapist actively helped her in this reconstruction process by believing her, by helping her explain how this memory might have been out of awareness for 20 years, and by encouraging her to expand on the moment at her daughter's bath by asking questions that might trigger further remembering. The memories developed in that therapeutic process led to a trial at which Eileen gave testimony that led to her father's imprisonment. (In 1996 the court decided to retry the case, given all the new findings about the questionable status of repressed memory, and George Franklin was set free.) Whatever that moment was like when Eileen first re-experienced a scene from the past, by the time she made that scene public it had been deeply influenced by the settings in which she made it public (first in her therapist's office and then in the courtroom). We have no way of knowing for sure what that original moment of memory was like for Eileen Franklin-Lipsker. It might have been just as vivid as she says or much more vague. It may be that she believes with everything in her the story she ended up telling. It is conceivable that she knows none of it is true. But the most likely scenario is that she absolutely believes the story as she came to tell it in therapy and in court. Whatever that first image or memory was at the side of her daughter in the bathtub, it is no more available to her for scrutiny than it is to us.

One of the most fascinating features of the courtroom as a setting for remembering concerns the role of the judge. It is the judge's job to be the impartial referee for the processes of constructing and using memories. In the role of referee the judge lays out what can only be called a theory of memory, what is otherwise known as instructions to the jury.

Look at the following, an excerpt from one judge's instructions to a jury. It shows the way in which the judge constructs the situation, particularly with regard to how the juries should hear and make sense of the memories people draw on in giving their testimony.

> Now your duty, jurors, is really the most important one here, and that is to find the facts and to render a verdict.
>
> Those of you who have had Latin should know that "verdict" comes from *veritas dicte*, and that means, "to speak the truth."
>
> You, the jurors, find the facts in this case and the lawyers, the parties, the judge, no one can stand in your shoes and make those determinations of the facts.
>
> Your decision about the facts is not subject to review. Anything that I do concerning rulings of law can be subject to review, but your decision, your verdict on the facts, is not subject to review.
>
> So find the facts as you, the jury, see fit to find them, and if there are conflicts in the evidence, it is your job to resolve those conflicts.
>
> One of the things that you will be doing also in finding the facts is assessing the credibility of the witnesses, but I'm getting a little ahead of myself.
>
> I want to tell you, jurors, that if during the course of the trial, if during my instructions to you now, or at any point you think that I have any views on this case, that I think it should come out one way or the other, please disregard that, because I have no view. I am not allowed to have any views, and I wouldn't presume to take away from you your responsibility. You are the ones who say what the view of the evidence is and what the view of the case is.
>
> So you're going to base your verdict, not upon what I have done, not upon what the lawyers have said in their openings or in their closing statements, but upon what the evidence is: and the evidence, as I said to you before, comes from a number of sources . . . the

sworn testimony of the witnesses who have appeared before you is evidence . . . [discussion with lawyers about the chemicals that are exhibits, etc.]. . . .

So that is the evidence in this case, and you are to base your verdict upon your considered evaluation of the evidence, and you will evaluate the evidence during your discussions, during your jury deliberations.

There are certain other things that are not evidence and that must not come into your deliberations.

Now I know none of you have read or heard anything about this case, but anything that occurs outside of the courtroom is not to enter into your considerations.

Your verdict is not a message to the community or a message to anyone else; it is a dispassionate view and analysis of what evidence was presented to you, and that's it. That's what your verdict is: nothing more and nothing less. You have enough to do that.

You must not allow sympathy to enter into your deliberations.

Now certainly it is obvious that Mr. Hickory is ill, and it's natural to have a feeling of sympathy for his illness and for his family's difficulties in that, and it is understandable to have those natural feelings, but they must not enter into your deliberations or into your verdict at all.

Likes or dislikes for a witness or for a lawyer or for a judge must also not enter into your verdict in terms of evaluation of the witnesses who testified before you.

Now there was some testimony by deposition transcripts, and you can evaluate that as you would any other witness in terms of, "Was that testimony reasonable or unreasonable; was it consistent with all of the other evidence, or was it inconsistent in a way that caused you to doubt the credibility of that testimony?" But deposition testimony has the same effect as other evidence. In other words you can accept it all or reject it all, or accept part of it, rejecting other parts.

Unlike the testimony of a witness who appeared before you, you don't have the opportunity to see that person and to evaluate that person; and the credibility of the witnesses is something that you will need to weigh in the case.

Now how do you do that? There are a number of ways or things that you can think about in evaluating the credibility of witnesses. And when I enumerate these factors, it is not at all an exclusive or totally exhaustive list, but you can think about the following things:

Consider the way the witness appeared on the stand. Did he appear to be frank or forthright. Or did he appear to be evasive or some other way? Was there something about the witness's demeanor that led you to believe or disbelieve his testimony? The evaluation of the credibility of somebody telling you something is really something that you do every day.

Usually you know the person, so you have some history and you know whether that person is credible or not. But in those situations where you don't know the person, you think of the other things to support your evaluation of that testimony.

You may consider all of the other evidence that you accept in determining the credibility of witnesses.

If a witness has said something different in a material, substantial way at another time — at a deposition, for example — you may consider that on the credibility of the witness. Because if somebody says "A" on the witness stand and not "A" in his deposition, then you may consider whether or not that affects your view of the witness's credibility.

You may also consider the intelligence that the witness shows: whether the witness has an interest in the outcome of the case; whether the witness seems to have any bias or motive in testifying.

You may also consider the opportunity that the witness had to observe the facts concerning which he testified  .  .  .  [instructions about expert witnesses].  .  .  .

You should bring your common sense into the jury deliberation room. You don't leave that behind you when you become a juror or when you are conducting your deliberations. So use your common sense in reaching your verdict in this case.

If I ordered anything to be stricken, or if I excluded testimony, you are not to concern yourselves with such matters that have been stricken or excluded.

Now in terms of evidence, there is direct evidence, and that is when somebody comes in and says, "Yes, I was there and I saw the motorist traveling 60 miles an hour in a 30-mile-an-hour zone." Direct evidence is something that a witness testifies to that he or she experiences with one of their senses, usually sight or hearing, but it can be other senses as well.

There is also indirect evidence, and that means that you are allowed to draw reasonable inferences from any facts that you find to be true.

An example of a reasonable inference would be if you left your house this morning and your mailbox was empty, and you returned this afternoon and there were letters and Christmas cards in your mailbox. You may reasonably infer from those two facts, even though you weren't there to see the postman, that the letter carrier came and delivered mail to your house.

The inferences that you draw must be reasonable. You wouldn't necessarily be able to say who the person was, the person's name, but you certainly are permitted to draw reasonable inferences from those facts which you accept to be true.

You may accept everything that a particular witness tells you lock, stock, and barrel. If you find that witness to be a credible witness and his testimony to be reasonable and believable, you may accept everything that is said and give that testimony whatever weight you want to give it in the overall picture of your verdict.

You may reject everything a witness says, and if you find that a witness has deliberately said something that was untrue in the past, you may consider that fact in rejecting all of the witness's testimony. You are not required to do so, but of course, you may; and you may also accept parts of the witness's testimony, rejecting other parts, and that applies equally to expert witnesses.

This set of instructions, while specific to this particular judge and case, contains much of what is usual in instructing juries about how to hear testimony and how to use that testimony. It presents a wealth of information about how the process of memory is constructed in the courtroom, including the internal contradictions within the instructions and instructions that seem to fly in the face of common, everyday memory practices. Let us examine these instructions.

The judge makes it clear that there are well-defined roles played in a courtroom. For instance, he stresses that though he will guide the overall proceedings (which might be analogous to what is, in more informal settings, known as a conversation about the past), he will have no opinion on the content of that conversation. This is quite different from everyday conversations in which each person clearly has a perspective of some kind and an openly vested interest, and no one person is in the role of guiding the discussion.

Moreover, the jurors are expected to make sense of various information without any motivation for it to come out one way or another. Recent memory research shows that we always construct the past in accordance with our current cognitive and affective needs, as well as our current affective state, or mood. The judge has structured—or would like to structure—memory activity in a way that flies in the face of people's everyday experiences of remembering.

There are some other notable features of the judge's instructions. He presents a conflict that is very important. On the one hand he stresses the importance of evaluating the reliability, or credibility, of a witness. The judge talks at some length about the difficulties of evaluating the reliability of people with whom you have no prior experience. At the same time, he underscores the importance of estimating their credibility in deciding whether to accept their testimony or not. Later he stresses that the jury can accept part of a witness's testimony and reject some other part. To begin with, the courtroom requires people to make judgments about other people's recollections based on almost none of the usual information we look for—the kind of information one gets over some length of time (how often a person has lied, or misremembered, how astute or honest a person tends to be, and the person's motivations in a given situation). So, on the one hand, jurors are presented with the unlikely task of evaluating a person's credibility based on almost no contextual information. But then the judge gives a conflicting injunction—that jurors can accept part of a person's testimony and reject other parts. While this instruction corresponds to the way memory really works (some recall is accurate and some is inaccurate, and any memory can be a bit of both), it is not how most people hear and evaluate one another's recollections. One of the distinctions the judge does not, and probably cannot, deal with is the difference between a witness who might be lying consciously, for a particular reason, and the witness who wants to tell the truth but distorts or misremembers unconsciously. Most of the time people consider another person's memories as either believable or not believable, even though a huge array of studies has now shown that we all forget, distort and misremember as a matter of course. Given this, it's more likely that jurors will follow the first part of the judge's instructions, the part in which he says they must decide if a witness is credible or not.

Another difference between courtrooms and other settings for memory is that the judge asks the jurors not to let context (mental, social, or environmental) shape what they think about what they hear. For instance, he urges them early in the instructions not to let anything they might know about the case, anything they hear or might have heard outside the courtroom, influence what they think about what they hear inside the courtroom. This runs counter to everyday behavior in which we judge each event, act, or conversation in terms of the schema we have already developed based on prior experiences. For instance, if your mother constantly paints the past more rosily than your recollection, you are going to use that information when judging any particular memory she insists upon. If you have a colleague at work who always embellishes the past in a way that puts him in a more important role than he actually played, you are going to keep that in mind as you consider any particular story he tells you.

The judge also urges the jurors not to let sympathy influence their verdict. And yet in most situations, our emotional responses to people, and our relationships with them, have a huge effect on what we do or don't believe about their recollections. For instance, when people are newly in love they are apt to believe everything their new lover tells them, even things that might seem incredible under other circumstances. When an adversary at work tells you something you don't like hearing, you are apt to disbelieve it, no matter how well it seems to fit the data. In other words, we use personal feeling, situational information, bias, and knowledge of individuals to evaluate recollection during almost all kinds of interactions that involve memory discourse. The courtroom is one well-defined and important setting in which memory is a salient and central mental and social activity, and in which it is constructed quite differently from ordinary memory.

The courtroom setting pressures people to think that a given memory is right or wrong, fact or fiction. If one part of the testimony can be shown to be fictional, none of it will be accepted as fact. When someone is shown to be completely wrong, he or she is thought of as either mentally deficient or intending to deceive (for instance, Kato Kaelin was perceived as untrustworthy in the O. J. Simpson trial proceedings). The understanding that a smart, competent person with the most honest intentions will still create the past in a somewhat idiosyncratic and erratic way is hard to tolerate in the courtroom setting. As one litigator says, "Jurors tend to think a witness is either reliable or unreliable. That's why it can be so effective to show that a witness has gotten even one small thing wrong. Because then the jurors are likely to believe that nothing that witness says can be counted on."

Almost completely absent from memory criteria in a courtroom setting are notions of nuance, evocation, and personal associations. Lawyers, judges, and jurors are not looking for the evocative detail of a remembered event, nor will they tolerate the notion of a subjective truth. An interesting point has been made about this by Neisser in his brilliant analysis of John Dean's Watergate testimony.

Dean gave his testimony about conversations in the Oval Office with President Nixon and others before anyone knew that those conversations had been tape-recorded by Nixon. Thus it was possible for Neisser to compare Dean's recollection (given in court testimony) with the actual transcripts of those conversations. Neisser shows that Dean got not only the facts wrong, but also the gist of the conversations as well. He argues that, instead, Dean got the meaning right. Until Neisser's paper on this testimony, psychologists thought that there were two levels on which a person could remember an event: they could recall both the sequence and the details or they could have forgotten specifics but accurately recall the gist, a kind of short summary of what happened. Neisser argues that the kind of mistakes Dean made in his testimony render his memory wrong at both levels. He got neither the gist of various conversations nor the sequence and details correct. However, Neisser shows that if you use Dean's recollections to construct a picture of Nixon, Haldeman, and Erlichman, and what their motivation and character were, as they became manifest across the conversations, Dean's memories of those conversations are correct. Neisser dubs this "repisodic memory," in contrast to the episodic memory psychologists talk about to describe a person's memory for a specific event or cluster of episodes. The term repisodic captures the fact that the conversations are recalled as if they were real episodes, with beginnings, middles, and ends marked in place and time. But unlike episodic memory, Dean's testimony collapses events across conversations and times, rendering them inaccurate as episodes but accurate for meaning. It was the accrual of those meanings across Dean's memories that is accurate, hence the repetition of certain details and nuance renders the truth of the events. Of course, this kind of inner meaning or truth is rarely considered acceptable or reliable by juries or lawyers.

Let's take another example. When a girl comes to court and accuses her father of sexual molestation, the implicit assumption is that the jury must find out if he touched her sexually or not. In this setting, the inner meaning of her memory is not the issue, though in therapy it might be. In court the question is whether someone should go to prison or not.

Courtrooms are a highly public and carefully structured setting in which remembering is often center stage in the proceedings. Everyone from judge, jury, witnesses, and lawyers to those of us who watch from a distance construes memory in a particular way to meet the requirements of the situation. We expect accuracy and verification; we look for consistency as a sign of truth, and inconsistency as a sign of distortion or lying. Our ability to remember will have a lasting impact on other members of the interaction. A trial is a highly ritualized social setting in which that most personal of all activities, remembering, is turned outward for the most public of uses. But there are other situations in which memory plays a central role and the process of memory is construed in particular ways. Not all situations strip memories down to their barest bones. Therapy, for instance, is a setting in which all players have strong, if implicit, theories of how and what to remember and how to use those memories. Consensus about the past has a whole different meaning in therapy than it does in the courtroom, and the reverberations or impact of a memory is more often than not internal rather than external.

## Therapy as a setting for collaborative remembering

Karen and Luis sit with the family therapist in his office. The therapist has asked both Karen and Luis to talk about their family of origin, as it is now carefully called, to distinguish it from the family one has created with a partner. Having done this over the past three sessions, the therapist is now suggesting that when Karen and Luis get into a quarrel, the problem is that they are projecting people, interactions, and relationships from the past on to one another rather than responding to the real, multidimensional person in front of them—the one they married. The therapist says to Luis, "You need to rid yourself of those ghosts. You are no longer a child, and the person in front of you isn't your mother. She's your wife." Karen stares at the therapist in surprise and remarks: "If we rid ourselves of those ghosts who will we be? I didn't come here to get rid of my ghosts or my past. I just wanted to know how those past relationships and interactions got me here. But not to lose those strands of me, or my memory." Luis chimes in sardonically, "Yeah, my mother- and father-in-law are part of my wife. Without them, she wouldn't be the woman I married." What they are discussing, in effect, is how their past influences who they are, and more fascinating, they are negotiating how to structure connections between past and present—how to use their memories.

Therapy is another setting in which memory tends to play a starring role. As in a courtroom, the participants in a therapy session tend to have strong theories about remembering and rememberers, whether those theories are implicit or explicit. For instance, in classic psychoanalytic therapy, remembering the past is supposed to lead to freedom from the chains of the past. In one of Freud's classic examples, a woman comes to him suffering from a persistent cough. Through analysis she finally remembers that while watching over her ailing father she felt restless and resentful, had fantasies that she needed to repress. That feeling made her so guilty that she coughed to distract herself from the forbidden thoughts. Now she coughs as a way of disguising her forbidden thoughts. Once she recalls the original event in which she coughed, the cough dissipates. Some view the classic psychoanalytic setting as a place where one reconstructs one's autobiography in order to become happier. In the analyst Roy Schafer's view this comes about from reconstructing one's memories to tell a happier story. Other psychotherapeutic approaches underscore the notion that you have to recognize the past relationships and people that inhabit or overshadow the present so that you can rid yourself of them. In each case, the therapist tries to help the patient view his or her past in a way that will help the patient live in the present.

What most modern talk therapies have in common is a belief in the idea that putting your past into words will have a positive impact on your present life. James Pennebaker's research clearly demonstrates the impact that articulating one's experience has on a person's health and well-being. For years he has looked at what happens when people tell or write about upsetting experiences and feelings. In general, his research shows that this kind of activity leads to fewer illnesses, fewer doctor visits, and a greater sense of well-being. Most recently, Pennebaker has examined the differences between communicating experiences and simply putting those experiences into words. He found that telling one's experiences to another person didn't lead to any greater health benefits than simply writing those experiences down. It seems that the process of putting past experience into a linguistic, possibly narrative form has a profound effect on how one functions and feels. The act of articulating an experience seems to transform the experience.

Not all therapies are alike, however. While all modern talk therapy has in common a belief in the value of articulating experience, the ways in which those articulations are used and the way in which the past is linked to the present differ in instructive ways.

Traditional psychoanalysis lies, in some respects, at one end of a continuum—a continuum that runs from those who believe that whatever a patient says in the context of therapy is true in some internal way to those who believe that therapy is a place for people to confront one another's versions of reality and adapt better to the reality that others perceive. In psychoanalysis, what a patient says about his or her past is of paramount importance. Some, like the analyst Donald Spence, would say that the analyst and patient create a text that can never reflect historical truth (some objective or consensual account of events). Instead, Spence claims that therapy only deals with what he calls narrative truth, which is as constrained by narrative values as it is by any kind of accurate memory. One implication of Spence's argument is that the therapist should never make the mistake of interpreting gestures or statements as statements of historical fact, but instead should always stay within the realm of the patient's emotional life and personal narrative. The psychoanalyst Roy Schafer would say that it is the reworking of that text that constitutes the therapeutic task. The therapist and patient strive to create and modify a story of the patient's life that in some way leads to greater happiness and adjustment. There is no way to check on the accuracy or reliability of the patient's recall. And to a great extent, what "really happened" is not significant. The assumption is that what is constraining or hampering the patient is the representation in his or her mind about what happened. The text he or she has created about the past is the only reality one can work on, at least from a traditional Freudian point of view. It is not the past, per se, but one's construction of the past that forms the material for therapy.

The recent psychoanalytic focus on narrative emphasizes the idea that experience itself can never be communicated directly. Mental experience, particularly when it directly taps unconscious thoughts, is kaleidoscopic, illogical, and often murky. Symbols and events can appear in a nonlinear fashion, almost impossible to communicate to another person. When talking to a therapist, the patient feels a strong pressure to put these unnameable thoughts and memories into a narrative form so as to make them coherent and communicable. Janet Malcolm characterizes this point of view: the patient is "always struggling with 'the conflict between what is true and what is describable.'" The true memory of dream or thought is often so unformed and murky and inchoate that it cannot be expressed except by resorting to narrative description, which somehow falsifies it. For it is in the very nature of speech to form, rather than to express, thought. "'The thought is in the mouth,' as Tristan Tzara once absently, unforgettably put it." Spence has argued that the relationship between patient and therapist heavily shapes the way in which the patient forms his or her thoughts into words and that this, as much as any direct representation of past experience, determines the meaning of what the patient says.

Early on in Freud's thinking, the idea was that the important past, the one the therapist must attend to, was the past re-enacted through transference. In other words, the patient plays out old dramas and relationships through the relationship constructed with the therapist. He or she "transfers" old dynamics onto this new stage. The real history is not clearly or simply what is conveyed through the patient's recollections and stories but rather is embedded in the interactions played out right then and there with the therapist, during the therapeutic hour. This kind of acting out and the analyst's focus on what is acted out, rather than what is recalled, are captured vividly in Daniel Menaker's *The Treatment*, which describes a young man's analysis with a Freudian, Ernesto Morales:

> Ten minutes after my session should have started, I pushed the buzzer outside the door of the brownstone in which Dr. Morales's office occupied the rear of the top floor, and he buzzed me in. In the stuffy, overheated waiting room, the noise machine, which like a Starship Enterprise gizmo, was hissing away. The machine could sound like anything — wind in a cane field outside Havana, a wave receding on a beach, a tiger's warning — but today it was just static. I looked out the window, which was flanked by two big flowerpots out of which *Cacti Freudii derelicti* thornily protruded. In the backyard of the house across the way, snow was building up on the back of the huge sow.

"Yes I know the story of this pig," Dr. Morales had said a few weeks earlier. "This was David Letterman's house, and he had this statue installed in the yard. And when he moved he did not take the pig."

"It's strange," I said.

"I agree," Dr. Morales said, "but what is even stranger to me is that you have not mentioned it before now. You have been coming three times a week for how long — two months now?"

"Four," I said. "But who's counting?"

"We shall get back to your anger in a moment," he said. "But right now perhaps you could talk a little about why you did not bring up such an odd thing for such a long time."

Morales takes the minute interactions within the therapy session as the text that represents his patient's psychic past as well as present. How the patient acts with the therapist, not what he says happened during his childhood, contains the true story. The idea here is that in the tiny interactions between patient and therapist—about what time the patient arrives, about the feelings the patient has about the therapist or believes the therapist has about the patient—the patient's past emotional and relational life is played out. In this psychoanalytic formulation the past is re-enacted within the confines of the therapeutic session. What the patient recalls about his or her life is simply a backdrop for the real memory, the one acted out, often unconsciously. The analyst makes a conscious narrative (interpretations) of the interactions within the therapeutic encounter. In this formulation, the memory as narrative is the one the analyst makes, not the one the patient recalls.

The problem with this formulation, concretized by Freudian analysts rather than Freud himself, is that one never can tell which aspects of the transference really capture something from the past. Moreover, with what we now know about the psychology of narratives, it is safe to assume that the narrative the patient creates through language is a deeply influential history, even if it is no less true to the past than the vagaries of transference.

Jerome Bruner has claimed that the narrative form directs our memory. If this is so, then the memory constructed in narrative is the psychic reality, or becomes so. In other words, the story one creates may not reveal what is revealed through transference. The narrative may never map perfectly onto some objective reality about the past. And yet the narrative not only communicates information to a therapist, it communicates information to the speaker. The story we tell others about our life gets incorporated into our self-image in such a way that it becomes as important a part of reality as external events.

In a fascinating case study two psychoanalysts, Ethel Person and the late Howard Klar, lay out for us in the case of one female patient some of the pitfalls and confusions that confront the Freudian analyst trying to disentangle "real" history from fantasies. They describe a woman with a fraught sexual history and a dissatisfying sexual and romantic adult life. She recalls an overbearing and judgmental father, but recalls very little about her mother. She specifically recalls a terrible evening when, as a teenager, she came home too late from a date and her father was very severe with her. After 120 sessions, the nature of her responses to the therapist intensifies in a dramatic way. The transference picks up speed, as it were. In the one hundred and forty-second session,

> The analyst dropped a pen on the floor, and as he bent over to retrieve it, the patient flinched noticeably on the couch. The analyst commented that she flinched as though she feared he would hit her. She blurted out, "If you touch me, I'll kill you." This moment was unlike any other in the analysis. The "as-ifness" of the transference evaporated, and her threat seemed to spring from a jack-in-the-box in which it had been long stored in her mind.

The analyst, upon reviewing his notes of the patient's recent transference behavior, her repetitive dream (of dancing naked in a circle of men, all of whom have erections; one of them—the analyst—is most interested and she has oral sex with him), says to her that day during the analytic session, "You behave like a person who has had something terrible happen to her. What happened here yesterday makes me wonder if you are struggling with some awful event you haven't yet been able to remember." What follows over the course of the next few months is the patient's discovery of a repressed memory that on that night when she came home late her father forced her to perform fellatio on him.

The paper is a thoughtful consideration of the problems analysts face in disentangling memory from fantasy. It is yet another approach to the question, raised in Chapter 2, of whether all recovered memories are based on real events. Person and Klar present an interesting hypothesis, again first constructed by Freud, that traumatic events, especially from childhood, are recalled with the body, whereas less traumatic events as well as experiences in adulthood are recalled with words and symbols. Thus, they conclude, early traumas are often more likely to show up through a re-enactment (transference) rather than a verbal memory. What is troubling about the authors' presentation, like so much other literature on this subject, is that they do not convince the reader that their patient did suffer the trauma the analyst helps her remember. There is no corroborating evidence outside of the vividness of the patient's recollection, the reality of her symptoms. It is almost impossible to distinguish, within the pages of their presentation at any rate, between what might have actually happened and what is a fantasy, created with the help of the therapist. I am not suggesting any intentional wrongdoing here; I mean only that in the murky waters of interpretation, the analyst who suggests a memory to a patient is participating so fully in the process of remembering that is hard to know what is what. Of course the consequences of therapy make all the difference.

In the case of the patient that Person and Klar describe, recovery of that memory didn't in itself change anything much except possibly the analyst's sense of the problem, which in turn influenced the patient and the direction the therapeutic encounters took. Regardless of what the therapist interpreted about the past, the patient still faced the task of building a new way of relating to men and of reworking her emotional connection to both her father and her mother. There is no suggestion, in the paper they wrote at any rate, that any fantasy or memory had a concrete impact on anyone's life outside the therapist's office. No one was accused or arrested of a crime. And no relationship was severed or reconstituted as a result of the recovered memory. I bring this up, because as I argued in the beginning of this chapter, the consequences of remembering vary greatly from one situation to another, and matter a great deal in thinking about what kind of truth a particular setting calls for. Persons and Klar point out the dangers involved in disentangling reality from fantasy, by quoting a fellow analyst, L. Josephs:

> The potential danger of [the analyst's] emphasis on the etiologic
> importance of actual events is that it might reinforce a defensive view
> of oneself as a passive victim of events which denies the patient's
> creative role in his adaptation . . . [but] . . . an emphasis on the

etiologic importance of wishes at the expense of actual events seems to suggest that patients are omnipotent in determining their intrapsychic reality and thereby denying human helplessness and limitation in the face of external reality.

In other words, if the analyst focuses too much on what "really happened" to a patient, he may be encouraging an unhealthy sense of victimization on the part of the patient, and at the same time underplay the patient's own responsibility in shaping her experience and behavior in daily life. On the other hand, if the analyst inflates the reality and significance of the patient's interpretation of life, with little regard for any external reality, he may show a damaging disregard for truly awful things that have happened to the patient over which she had little or no control.

Thus the dilemma for psychoanalysts and their patients concerns what to make of what is said about the past. Do the memories that people construct within a therapeutic setting represent what really happened? Some, like Donald Spence, would argue that the real issue concerns the narrative reality that is represented. Others, like Person and Klar, would argue that the past is re-enacted, and any narrative must be constructed on the basis of that enactment rather than a narrative the patient produced. In other words, do the therapist and patient work together, building a life story for the patient? Or is the story implicit in the patient's behavior (inaccessible to the patient's conscious mind)? Must the story of what has happened to a patient lie dormant until a therapist interprets actions displayed within the therapeutic hour to become an actual story of the past? In the first view, the patient comes and sits down in therapy to tell about the time his mother made him get out of the car on a highway and stand alone while she drove off—punishment for acting wild. The therapist's task then is to explore the meaning of this story, connect it to other stories, and use it as a way of building a happier story about the present. In the second view, this kind of story is peripheral and untrustworthy. Instead, the same patient may well reveal his sense of loneliness and lack of trust in loved ones through his responses, silences, and withdrawals during therapy.

What both views accept is that the construction of the past that occurs in psychoanalytic settings is a highly creative one. That is, patient and doctor are making a story of the past, not simply recording objective facts. In both views there is an implicit notion of authorship, though how that role is filled differs from one theorist to another.

Psychoanalysts agree that the most important use of the past is to illuminate the present, though they might differ on how that past is unearthed and how closely the constructed past reflects an actual past. In addition, these psychoanalysts agree, explicitly or implicitly, that the alleviation of symptoms is an answer in itself. Whether any given memory represents inner or outer reality is not clear, however. When a patient's cough disappeared, Freud took that as evidence that he had helped her uncover a powerful event from the past. The event was, in the first place, psychic rather than actual. One way to view the Freudian perspective on this topic is to see it as a kind of a pragmatic approach to memory. It matters less whether something really happened, and more that the representation of past events be used to free one from present constraints. In other words, a debate within the field centers on whether narratives or transference itself lead to knowledge of the past. This debate also concerns the capability of therapists to know what really happened. But psychoanalysts do agree that whatever past is constructed or interpreted in therapy is valid if uncovering it leads to a happier life.

Not all therapy focuses so intensely on uncovering the past and not all therapy focuses so much on the uncorroborated internal construction of the individual patient. At the other end of the psychotherapeutic continuum is the family therapy model. In these settings when individuals construct their past they have to confront other people's constructions of those same events. The interactions form a kind of text (the interpreted transference in the Freudian setting) for a therapist to interpret. But often the therapist's goal is actually to change ways of interacting among family members. For instance, in a well-known example from the groundbreaking family therapist Salvatore Minuchin, the therapist encourages two parents of an anorexic girl to force her to eat, right then and there in the family therapy session. In albeit extreme examples like this, the past is left implicit and the current dynamics are in some way nudged, rearranged, elicited, or jarred by the therapist's actions. In other words, the therapist works on whatever actions and interactions are occurring right there in front of him (in this case, the girl's refusal to eat and the parents' difficulty responding to this refusal). His focus is on changing those interactions rather than using them as a guide to the past that in turn will transform the present.

On the other hand, in many family therapy settings, the therapist wants to get a story or set of stories about the past, and the various family members find themselves either constructing a shared story about why they are in therapy or confronting differences in the way they remember what has been happening at home. The therapist can help the clients come to some agreement on the past, some shared representation of what happened. Or she can treat their disagreement as the material on which to work. She may also try and get them to accept the idea that each of them experienced a given episode in a different way and that, in fact, there can be different constructions of the same event.

In the following therapy example, family members disagree about what has happened. And that disagreement forms the crux of the issue, or what is known from a more literary point of view as the problem in the story. The father, stepfather, mother, stepmother, and suicidal teenaged daughter, Faith, are meeting with a family therapist.

> DR. FISHMAN (to no one in particular): So what do you all think about this?
>
> MOTHER: Well, she's here to get help, and the family session is part of the treatment, is my understanding.
>
> DR. FISHMAN: Now what is it that has occurred?
>
> MOTHER: I think Faith should answer that. Since she's the one who took the pills, she should say why she did it or . . .
>
> DR. FISHMAN: Then why don't you ask Faith why she did it?
>
> MOTHER: Why did you take the pills?
>
> FAITH: Because I thought you guys were putting me down a lot, and—I don't know—it seemed like you just didn't like me being around and stuff, and I just, I didn't like that, so I just thought, well, if it happens, I die, and if it doesn't—I don't know.
>
> STEPFATHER: By "putting you down" do you mean telling you to do your homework and turn the TV off at 10:30 at night and stuff—is that putting you down?

Later in the same session, the therapist tries to "provoke change in this system." That is, he tries to guide members of the family toward doing at least one thing differently, to shake up the patterns of interaction. He does not focus, per se, on getting them to agree or understand the past.

> DR. FISHMAN: It seems to me the difficult part is that the adults aren't exactly clear on the way to approach Faith on what's best

for Faith. During the course of a month she spends time with everybody and clearly you have differences. What Faith needs so she won't feel so confused and so she won't feel somehow criticized, is that all of you agree.

STEPFATHER: Well, let me rephrase my question. (To Faith): If you're doing the best you can, and you get a C that's okay with me.

FAITH: Then Mom says that if I get a C, I have to take seventh grade over.

MOTHER: When did I say that?

FAITH: This year.

MOTHER: Yes. The first semester we did not question her about what she was doing, other than occasionally ask do you have any homework, what did you do in school. We didn't know how she was doing until after she got her report card. But sometime in January we became aware of the cutting school problem. And it was pointed out to her that you cannot get away with it. So we cracked down on her this semester. (To Faith): And you know that, don't you? We didn't bug you at all last semester, did we? Think about it.

The mother and daughter disagree on how to construct these events. There is no question that certain events happened, but the description of the events comes about through contradictions, not through the kind of collaborative dialogue that you might see, for instance, between parents and their 2-year-old, in which there is virtually no verbal disagreement about what has happened in the past.

When Faith reports that her mom threatened her with a repeat of seventh grade if she got a C, the mother counters, "When did I say that?" as if it might not have happened. When Faith answers the question literally (by telling her when she said it), the mother agrees and goes on to expand on why she said it, changing the meaning of her actions by setting them in a justifying context. So they come to agree on an event and communicate to others, but only through a conflict-ridden dialogue.

Much of the time families (especially the ones who have been motivated to get professional help) construct the past through their disagreements. Each version is what Andrus Prok calls the blank page method of lying. He contrasts this with the direct lie method, which is a simple falsification. On the other hand, the blank page method is when verifiable facts are selected and arranged to create an "overall distorted picture." All of us use the blank page method of lying when constructing our past. (How people do this in their autobiographies is discussed in Chapter 5.) But there are particular reverberations when several members of a family each use the blank page method of lying to talk about the same event and do so in front of one another. In the case of Faith and her family, confronting one another's construction of the past, or blank page lies, furthers the therapy.

Sometimes, as in the case that follows, family members in therapy draw on more than one layer of their autobiographical memory. The mother and father both believe that therapy is a place not only to relate what has been happening in the recent past but also how those memories might be connected to their individual memories of the long-ago past. The therapy becomes an occasion for weaving together what they each remember, what they know of one another's memories, and what they have experienced together more recently. In the follow- ing case, a husband, wife, and children are in therapy; the central problem is incest between the father and the 12-year-old daughter, who is not present in this session. Neither are the two boys. The 2- year-old daughter is in another room. In the room with the husband and wife are the 14-year-old daughter and the father's mother.

DR. FISHMAN: How can we help?

FATHER: Yeah, I guess, it's been rough. I guess I growed up in a bad way or something, I don't know. Different things happen in my life. I don't know what I'm really looking for or anything like that. It's been—the past four months—it's been kind of mixed up and everything.

As the therapy unfolds, it's clear that the husband and wife both see his own childhood experiences (including abuse) as the basis for his abuse of their daughters. So the story they construct about what is happening in their own home rests on the story they have constructed about what happened in their own childhood. In this sense, they, like the judge in court, have a theory about how memory works and how it should be used.

In each of the therapeutic settings discussed here, the therapist comes with an idea about how the patient and the therapist should use the past. In each case the patient will be guided toward some orienta- tion about the past, maybe similar to, maybe different from, the naive or implicit view of the past with which she or he came into the office. In all cases memory is not only the image or picture the patient walks into the office with but also an attitude toward what memory is, what role it will play in the therapy. In addition, memory in a therapeutic setting consists of those representations that are created with a therapist. These constructions may or may not build on what the individual brings into the room. For instance, you come to the therapist's office with a specific memory of yourself as a young child playing with your little sister. It is often the case that out of that simple-seeming scene you and the therapist construct a much more complex scene, similar to going from a photograph to a video. This is not to suggest that the memory you construct during therapy is false or that the input of the therapist distorts or contaminates the memory. Quite the opposite. This is what memory is in the everyday world of social interaction. It is the transformation of what may begin as an internal private moment into something larger and more layered, something that bears the imprint and influence of those around you. In therapy, the goal, which is personal happiness or freedom from psychological symptoms, shapes remembering. The therapist and patient (or patients) are looking to construct a past that will both explain and improve the present situation.

In the courtroom, the past is used to find who is at fault for misdeeds and who is not. The repercussions of the memories constructed in a courtroom are quite concrete and public: jail, fines, and freedom. The goal of therapy, on the other hand, is the alleviation of psychological symptoms, or more generally, greater personal and family happiness. Both are settings in which the goal influences what is and is not acceptable as a memory, how much value is placed on objective truth, and how much value is placed on uncovering the meaning of a memory. What the two settings share is the highly articulated nature of memory. We come to both settings ready to draw on our memories or to make judgments about the memories others communicate. We apply implicit theories of the structure of memories as well as how we think we might use those memories. Court proceedings and therapy both transform memories from a private, internal experience to the stuff of transaction. Both settings require people to articulate the past, share it, and build memories in response to specific requests and directions. And in both settings the personal past becomes part of the social domain, drawing the rememberer into closer contact with others.

CHAPTER FOUR
# THEN AND NOW: CREATING A SELF THROUGH THE PAST

Ideas and memories are the most intimate part of man, where nobody can scrutinize, where not even the harshness of the mountain can penetrate — the only thing that nature cannot easily transform. You nourish your memories, and when you lie down in your hammock at night you hold your memories close to you; you bring them out a bit into the world, you turn them over in your head, you parade them a bit, timidly in front of your eyes, though you never really see them. So you air these memories, and before going to sleep you return them very slowly to your brain, as if back into a spiral shell that is very gradually closing. You wind in your ideas once again, and probably your body curls up, too, I don't know — you start to gather in your ideas, to reel in your memories until they are all covered over and perfectly quiet, in the shelter of your brain, as if resting — and you sleep. You might say that the only umbilical cord, the only thread that still binds you to that past, or to that present which has become the past, is idea, memory.

—Omar Cabezas

In almost all the examples I've described until now, whatever germ of remembrance that begins as a totally internal and private moment is shaped and transformed by the social exchange through which it becomes materialized. And yet, one doesn't simply send a memory out into the world, and remain unaffected by the self-in-the-past communicated to others. Whether it's with a lover, a lawyer, or a therapist, the self described in a memory becomes incorporated, if only temporarily, into one's current sense of self. It travels from the inner reaches of the mind out into the world and then is folded back again into one's identity. What we recall of our earlier selves, and why, are matters of great empirical and theoretical debate. How those remembered selves relate to the current one doing the remembering is of equal importance.

If it is true that remembering is a process of transforming an internal moment of re-experiencing into something one shares with other people, the next step is to understand how these shared memories (testimony, therapy, conversations with friends) help to construct a self.

It has become fashionable of late, almost too comfortably so, to assume that we know how our remembered selves create our current self. At least 30 books have been written in recent years focusing on the ways in which we each construct ourselves through our memory. And yet, from an empirical point of view, it's not at all clear that there is one way, or even one model, that accounts for how the selves of the past are related to the current self. Consider, for instance, the experience of searching for the perfect anecdote to tell a friend, one that will convey to your friend what a tense and competitive relationship you've always had with your sister. You already know the meaning, the theme that you want to share, and what you have to do is scan your collection of illustrative personal stories to find the best one. Now contrast this with the experience of being told by a friend that every story you've ever told about your work ends the same way: that you have been the victim of unfair and unwarranted prejudice and malice by colleagues. In this case you conveyed a theme, without even knowing you were doing it.

And both of these spontaneous uses of memory differ from deliberate efforts to create a self through writing or telling one's life story. Many writers have explicitly announced to the reader that the purpose of their memoir is to connect their past self to their present self. The urge to write is an urge to find purpose, explanation, and meaning in one's life events. In her memoir, *Family Sayings*, the Italian essayist Natalia Ginzburg begins to identify themes of her family life while growing up, which could only emerge in the context of writing for an audience. For example, early in the memoir Ginzburg lists things that her father liked—socialism, England, Zola's novels, the Rockefeller Foundation—and things her mother liked—socialism, Paul Verlaine's poetry. Ginzburg goes on to recount one of her mother's childhood memories of walking down the street in Milan and seeing a large man standing in front of a hairdresser's window, whispering, "Lovely, lovely." And goes on to talk about how much of her mother's memories are built on remembered phrases she had heard. Thus the author's past is constructed through the act of writing.

The extreme version of creating meaning, sequence, and theme in one's life story through the telling of it occurs when people create an autobiography of a life never lived. Take, for example, the startling case of Binjamin Wilkomirski, whose devastating account of living his early years (ages 3 to 10) in concentration camps during World War II reads as if it is the most direct, bleak, and vivid account possible of that world seen through a child's eyes. The memoir even displays the disjointed and chaotic quality that would seem appropriate for long-stifled memories from early childhood. And yet, recent discoveries suggest that Wilkomirski fabricated his account, that in fact he did not live the life he depicted. Explanations of this kind of phenomenon are fascinating in themselves. (Does he believe what he wrote? If not, why did he, probably correctly, think a memoir would be more popular than an admittedly imagined account?) But the point in the present context is that whether false or true, for some, telling their life story is a means of finding continuity between past and present. What all these examples have in common is that the self created through memories was shaped by the situations in which an inner experience was shared with others.

Some situations lead us to draw deliberately on the past to convey who we are, while in other settings the creation of a self can emerge when we least expect it.

## The self as personal historian

We each believe ourself to be our own personal historian. We record events from the past, and dredge up others that we thought long since lost or buried. We start doing this as early as age 3. As Jerome Bruner, among others, has pointed out, it is clear that we do this instinctually. It seems to be an intrinsic part of being human to organize past experience and use it again and again.

The literary critic Daniel Albright suggests that we recall the past to understand and justify who we are. He casts this in a framework that I think extends to all of us when he says, "Psychology is a garden, literature is a wilderness." He argues that psychologists' goal is to cure people. They want to create coherence in order to allow people to figure out what their memories mean. For the research psychologist, this means finding patterns and predictability in what people recall and how they recall. For the clinical psychologist, this means knowing how to help others interpret the past so that patients can be freed from those elements in their memories that bind them in their current life.

Writers, on the other hand, want to justify, and use the past to explain who they are, Albright argues. If you take a literary approach to thinking about memory, you are more likely to find idiosyncrasy rather than pattern, individuality rather than generalizations. The writer and the literary critic, in other words want the past to entertain, engage, and perhaps illuminate the narrator, and by extension or identification, the reader.

It is most likely that in everyday life most of us are part writer and part psychologist. We all use the past to justify who we are, but also to know and perhaps change or overcome who we were. We all have implicit theories regarding the patterns and logic of memory, and at the same time are immersed in the unpredictable specificity of our own memories and remembering experiences.

Whether one uses the past to justify or transcend one's past, whether one views memory as predictable and explainable or murky and idiosyncratic, we draw upon memories as a source for the present. We dig out, amplify, and create autobiographical material as a way to know and communicate who we are now. But most often, this archaeological work happens in the company of others, even when those others are representations in our mind. Thus the internal work of creating coherence and meaning out of memories is never done in a social vacuum. We are always remembering in the company of others.

At age $2\frac{1}{2}$, my youngest son, Sam, has discovered the power, and thus the meaning, of telling stories about things that have happened to him. He is as interested in stories he cannot remember as those he can. The urge appears to be simultaneously social and internal. He is creating a self for himself as he creates one for others.

He overhears me talking about the time when he was a newborn baby and his eldest brother, Jake, slipped down the stairs while holding him. How does he know this is an interesting story? What about the story is interesting to him? What flags it as a candidate for his autobiographical repertoire? He asks me to tell it over and over again. He tries to tell it to others, and then turns to me, asking me to fill in, end it, and add to it. Researchers have found that it is common for 2-year-olds to collaborate with others (usually parents) in telling stories about their past.

He turns to an adult friend and begins, "When I was a born baby . . . (hesitation while he tries to find the words) Jake was holding me. And he fell, and he cried, and . . . (turning to me), Mommy, you tell the rest?" He wants to have that memory, and by telling the story he is trying to create it as a memory for himself. Equally, he wants to have a story to tell others—he is performing his memory for an audience.

What makes it a good memory for him? It is dramatic. It involves a fall and fear. Jake cried and assured me that the baby wasn't hurt. It involves action and emotion. Sam plays a central role. And everything comes out all right. It makes a good story, and a perfect one to fit into his emerging autobiography. He not only is a central character in the memory, but the memory demonstrates his powerful connection with a family member and the powerful effect their experience had on other family members. At this point in his life, Sam's personal stories don't fit together into an autobiography. At this age toddlers collect autobiographical memories. Not only do they not offer memoir-like narratives, they also are unable, even upon request, to tell their life story. It is not even clear that they have any sense of acquiring a collection of stories about the self.

All the young rememberer is capable of is choosing interesting episodes to repeat, edit, and embellish. My son, like many toddlers, seems motivated to tell stories as a meaningful activity in and of itself (aside from the intrinsic interest of the specific information or material). But he does not view his life retrospectively. Nor can he tell you about events in his life on demand or with any kind of order, either temporal or thematic. This is not to say that his stories don't begin to contribute to his self-concept. They do. But in the first few years of life the connections between memories, the emerging themes, and the lines from early life to present life are not conscious. There is no evidence to suggest that young children have any explicit awareness of autobiography, life story, or even the ways in which their past experiences are tied to their current life. But the dimensions and nature of our remembering processes undergo dramatic change in the first 10 years of life.

The sheer capacity of our memory expands during early childhood. A 10-year-old can recall more items on a list than a 4-year-old can. What is perhaps more important is that children become more conscious of their own memory, more deliberate about how and what they recall. When preschoolers are asked to remember a list of words or other quantity of information, they appear to do nothing special to aid their own memory. Older children use specific strategies, such as repeating the list to themselves over and over again, chunking the information in groups, or using simple mnemonic devices. The development of other important cognitive processes during this period also has a substantive effect on the way people remember. For instance, Sylvia Scribner and Michael Cole have shown that literate and nonliterate children differ in their tendency to use organizing strategies to help them with memory tasks. Conceptions of the self have been shown to relate to how likely people are to talk about individual experiences from the past.

While there has been great interest in fledgling attempts by toddlers to recall and recount past experience, and considerable interest in the character and function of life stories in adulthood, only a handful of studies have looked directly at how children first tell their life story. It appears that children first share incidents about their past with parents, then with teachers, then peers. When an experimenter asks 7-year-olds to tell their life story, it is a novel task for them. Children range widely in how they approach the activity, from describing in detail the story of their birth to talking only about what has happened in the preceding 4 months. The sense of a ready-made life story, the kind an adult might offer upon demand (to a date, to a therapist, in an interview) doesn't seem available to children under the age of 12.

Sam, for instance, doesn't yet have an implicit or explicit theory of his own remembering. His memories have not yet become objects for reflection. Nothing about his behavior (or that of any toddler observed in any study) suggests that he thinks about what his memories mean, how they relate to who he is, or anything about how he comes to recall what it is he recalls. And yet, autobiographical novels and autobiographies are replete with reflections on the memory process itself. It is not simply our memories and memory processes that develop. Not only do we develop an awareness of our own memory process, this awareness becomes integral to how and what we recall.

Sam, at $2\frac{1}{2}$, is just realizing both the power and meaning of autobiographical memories. The memories are powerful for him internally because they give him an intoxicating, and necessary, sense of personal continuity—what Ulric Neisser refers to as the extended self. The extended self is the sense that "I exist over time, and the same me was at the birthday party, falling down the stairs, eating cotton candy, going to the doctor, and it's the same me who is sitting here now thinking about all of that." This is probably one of the great epistemic discoveries one makes in life, similar in impact to the discovery that everything has a name. It is the dawning awareness of the experiencing "I" that William James talks about. It is the awareness of consciousness. The child is at first a remembering self, looking with admiration and interest at all his or her remembered selves, at the same time discovering and exploiting his or her capability to portray that self to others.

## The remembering self and the remembered self

From his or her first autobiographical references, the young child experiences a bifocal view of the past: the self looking backward and the selves one sees in the past. The interplay among these selves is one of the most interesting dynamics that researchers, and everyone else who reflects on their memories, confront. Penelope Lively's memoir, *Jacaranda, Oleander* (discussed in Chapter 1), exquisitely captures the double vision implicit in the adult memory of childhood experience:

> We are going by car from Bulaq Dakhrur to Heliopolis. I am in the back. The leather of the seat sticks to my bare legs. We travel along a road lined at either side with oleander and jacaranda trees, alternate splashes of white and blue. I chant, quietly: "jacaranda, oleander . . . jacaranda, oleander. . . ." And as I do so there comes to me the revelation that in a few hours' time we shall return by the same route and that I shall pass the same trees, in reverse order — oleander, jacaranda, oleander, jacaranda — and that, by the same token, I can look back upon myself of now, of this moment. I shall be able to think about myself now, thinking this — but it will be then, not now.
>
> And in due course I did so, and perceived with excitement the chasm between past and future, the perpetual slide of the present. As, writing this, I think with equal wonder of that irretrievable child, and of the eerie relationship between her mind and mine. She is myself, but a self which is unreachable except by means of such miraculously surviving moments of being: the alien within.

There is not simply one line of connection, one explanation for how the remembering self corresponds or creates links with the remembered selves. The remembering self is always a person in a specific situation, remembering for a particular reason. I recall my childhood in the company of good friends, eager to show them how outrageous I was as a child, or I recall an incident in anger and rage, eager to show my parent how unhappy I used to be, or I write about my early years as a way of explaining how I became a writer, and so on. Penelope Lively recalls her jacaranda chant as a way of opening her memoir of her childhood in Egypt during World War II. She at once gives you a sensuous experience of where she lived, the conditions of her childhood, and a way into her inner life. Why a person recalls what he or she does is shaped by the setting in which person recalls. But it is also true that the way in which past and present selves are connected is shaped by the context of remembering as well. By context I mean both the form the memory takes (written, spoken in conversation, spoken in therapy) and also the mental context—what else one is talking about and why.

What are some of the ways in which the remembering self and the remembered self meet, and how do other people participate in this process? Most moments of remembering are not done alone in the process of self-understanding or self-contemplation. Many personal recollections that contribute to one's identity unfold in highly motivated and charged situations—where there are other people. You are trying to justify yourself, impress another person, show how you are the same, or different, from others. These situations then end up shaping one's life story as it emerges across time and place. In this way context plays a huge role in determining the self one knows through one's stories about the past. A colleague tells of the time his young daughter came home from her first day of school. He asked her how it was. "Not good," she said. "Really," my colleague replied, looking concerned. "What was bad about your day?" "The teacher made me spend the day in the closet." "Sophie, did that really happen?" he asked. "No," she said, looking serious and upset, "but it could have."

This poignant example demonstrates a common dynamic in memory exchanges. The past we describe is often determined more by unconscious feelings that are real even when not located in the events we recount, and our need to justify a feeling, to convince someone of something. Sophie may have been anxious about school. Perhaps her story reflects an important fantasy. Equally probable, her story had the effect on her listener that she wanted. It elicited from her father sympathy and collusion, a belief that her experience warranted her worried feelings about school. The tendency to use the past to convince others of one's construction of reality is even more pervasive and perhaps more problematic as we become adults. It may also be harder to detect, less flagrant when adults tell each other about the past.

A life story is usually a patchwork affair, unless you are an author, or perhaps, a politician. For most of us, different stories come out at different times; some are repeated until they are well-rehearsed yarns, while others may tumble out before one even knows what they are meant to signify. And the stories only cohere as a unified autobiography in the most subtle, inchoate way. In fact, most of the time people recall a story at a time, or a string of stories, rather than *the* life story. These stories may contain or stand for much more than the specific incident being recounted.

Often a particular reminiscence acts as a template, standing for a whole strand of feeling or events in one's life. These templates can provide a stage on which to experience a form of transference. In other words, we then project onto that memory all the feelings and thoughts that we have toward a multitude of experiences and emotions for which it stands. The template memory, like the psychotherapist, becomes a stand-in for a set of unresolved feelings we cannot confront directly. A particular feeling or idea that has followed one through life is encapsulated in a given story. Telling it evokes the reactions and images that actually occurred across myriad incidents and events.

At other times, there is a strong urge to tell a sequence, a chronology of one's life events. But again, this is most often done in response to a particular social situation or interpersonal dynamic. Choosing and connecting specific happenings to create one's life narrative is usually done to satisfy very specific psychological and social purposes.

Finally, there are people who deliberately use the process of autobiography to re-create themselves. Again, this is at heart a response to being with others, and thus is best explained in interpersonal as well as intrapersonal terms. We all know of people, both privately and in the public domain, who create a persona that may turn out to be far different from whom they used to be. The most obvious examples of this are writers who convey a self through their published works that seems far different from the self they display in personal interactions. It is typical for people such as this to choose autobiographical information that supports the self they want to present to the world. But it is also true that this self-creation through selective memory is done with and for other people.

In each of these cases, two seemingly opposing forces are at work.

On the one hand is a person's need to experience him- or herself as continuous across time (the extended self). And on the other hand is the tremendous motivation to present what Erving Goffman calls a face, a particular self that fits the current social situation and elicits satisfying social feedback. Most personal reminiscences bear the influence of these two forces. Those reminiscences, in turn, circle back and feed the constantly shifting inner self. Thus the self is shaped, at least in part, by the vagaries of the situations in which one recalls the past.

## Self for self and self for others

If we draw on our memories to create an ongoing sense of who we are in the present, how does this self for self relate or conflict with the different selves in the past we describe for others?

The sociologist Erving Goffman has described the ways in which we create different faces, or selves, in response to different social situations. He illustrates the ways in which people collude in helping you to maintain a given face, or self-presentation. One of the ways we support or maintain these faces is to draw on memories that support the self we are presenting to others. In this way the self we construct through memory may shift to fit different social situations. For instance, when I am around family I am likely to tell stories about how strange I was as a child. This fits the family stereotype of me and fulfills my need to be seen as eccentric. It may also fulfill more subtle family dynamics. It may be a form of ingratiation, a way of pleasing my siblings by "one-downing" myself. On the other hand, when I am in an adversarial position on our local school committee, I am likely to tell stories about my past that illustrate my superior achievements, strengths, and skills as an educator. I may want to cow my colleagues and convince them I am an authority. Goffman argues that we present a face in each social setting, a self-for-others. Those others collude with us, helping us to maintain the self, or line, that we have established.

For instance, one might want to present oneself as lighthearted and easygoing. In that case, not only your way of talking and your manner, but also the stories you tell about yourself, highlight your lightheartedness. Those around you will help you maintain that face. They won't tend to challenge your stories but instead will give you feedback that deepens or strengthens your self-presentation. You are likely not only to choose stories that illustrate your lightheartedness but to tell about the past in a way that suppresses your serious side and underscores your easygoing side. In this way two different selves emerge in two different settings, each one connecting a line between different collections of memories.

And yet, we work hard to create and maintain a sense of inner cohesion and consistency in our self-concept. This is, to a large degree, what cognitive dissonance theory is all about. Elliot Aronson refined the theory of cognitive dissonance and made it even more applicable to the study of autobiographical memory. He argued that we are particularly vulnerable to cognitive dissonance and its reduction when the conflict between a thought and an action or two contradictory thoughts involves our self-concept: we like to think of ourselves as good, decent people, and we like to believe we are consistent over time and across situations. Thus, any time our actions and/or beliefs threaten our self-concept as good, decent, smart, and consistent, our dissonance reduction mechanisms go into high gear. We reconstruct reality in a way that restores our self-concept. Aronson uses the example of smokers trying to deal with the plethora of information that shows that smoking is bad for you. How does one deal with the dissonance between the belief that you are smart, on the one hand, and the evidence that you are doing something that is stupid? Aronson suggests these three options:

> You quit smoking.
>
> You convince yourself there is no proof that smoking is bad for you.
>
> You say, "I'd rather live the way I want to even if it means I live briefly."

Comparatively few people choose the first. It is easier to construct an added argument that somehow closes the gap between the action and the belief (in this case, that I am a smart person and I smoke). The theory was not cast particularly as a theory of memory, but in fact this theory often can explain why people describe their past in the ways that they do.

To take a recent example, when the journalist Jon Krakauer recounts his participation in the disastrous 1996 climb up Mt. Everest in *Into Thin Air*, he needs to explain his contribution to the death of fellow climber Andy Harris in such a way as to maintain his self-concept as a decent and responsible person. He does this by highlighting his own altitude sickness, his exhaustion, and his difficulty with the cold after his struggle down the mountain during a storm, and his mistaken belief that he saw Harris precede him into the safety of the campsite. In this way he constructs the past in such a way that his dissonance is reduced. It would be the rare circumstance in which a person would recall an event from the past and say, "I was just a terrible person at that moment."

As another dramatic example, take Robert Jay Lifton's examination of Nazi doctors and their recollections of their murderous work in the concentration camps of the late 1930s and 1940s. Their accounts provide mammoth rationalizations of how one could have taken the Hippocratic Oath and then devote one's medical skills to torture and murder. In each case the doctor explained the seeming contradiction by reconstructing the surrounding boundaries of reality (Jews were gangrene of the body of mankind, and in order to save mankind, we had to remove the gangrene). In a few cases the doctors could not reduce dissonance this way, and ended up alcoholic, insane, or a suicide. No one simply said, "In that situation, at that time, I was a terrible person who did terrible things and so that is a part of who I am." Few people simply live with the feeling of dissonance, and memory provides us with an extraordinarily creative and potent tool for reducing dissonance about ourselves.

The social psychologist Anthony Greenwald has shown how the ego dominates the construction of events such that one's own role is not only placed at the center of an event, it is recalled in such a way as to maintain a positive and consistent self-concept. We know, for instance, that people tend to overestimate their own contribution to a group effort (if five people work on a project, each of them will estimate their part as being more than one-fifth of the total effort).

Dissonance theory (and the many experiments it has spawned) helps explain why and how we recall the past in ways that shape our current sense of self. We change past experiences so that they confirm how we see ourselves in the moment. We want to know that in the past we were good and intelligent, and that there is some consistency between how we have acted and the self-presentation we offer in the present.

This brings us to a fascinating paradox inherent in the process of remembering the self. On the one hand, dissonance theory predicts (correctly) that we recall the past in a way that makes us seem and feel consistent. On the other hand, Erving Goffman has convincingly argued that there is no one self we present across all situations, that in fact we present different selves to suit different contexts.

One might say that the process of remembering oneself in the past is shaped by two opposing forces: the motivation to construct a consistent self and the motivation to re-create the self to fit differing social situations. Rather than choosing between these forces as explanations for how we recall ourselves in the past, it seems more fruitful to say that memories of one's past are a result of the way in which these contrasting forces shape a given moment of remembering. For instance, imagine that your teenaged daughter has asked you about your sex life when you were a teenager. You worry that your daughter feels bad that she doesn't have a boyfriend, that she thinks she is the only 15-year-old in the world who has never slept with a man. You want to describe yourself as having been shy and inexperienced at that age. The situation calls for a particular description of that period of your life. But you are someone drawn to describing yourself as wild, full of life and adventure; it is your tendency to choose those episodes in your past that illustrate your daring and sometimes foolish penchant for excitement. What will you tell your daughter? Probably a story that contains shades of both forces: in some ways your story will reveal your love of excitement even as a 15-year-old, and yet, will end with a view of you as similar to her: shy and inexperienced. You might achieve this by making the outer landscape one of loneliness ("We lived in the country, honey, and my parents were strict: I rarely went out. I really didn't know that many boys"), and of inner wildness ("But I was very restless, I read lots of romance books, and made eyes at every guy who walked through the house").

But these two ends of a continuum (the past for the self and the past for others) don't tell the whole story. In addition, there are different kinds of autobiographical memories, and each reflects a particular approach to knowing oneself through one's past.

As the field of memory research has grown, there has been a veritable smorgasbord of findings about various features of autobiographical memory and the factors that constrain and direct what and how we recall the personal past. We know that one can recall oneself in an event or as an onlooker to an event. One can recall only the good things about one's past or the bad things that prove the rule. You can recall the details correctly or you can miss details but get the overall gist right. You can get the gist wrong but accurately convey the meaning of the event. You can be more likely to recall a sequence or you can be more likely to convey the visual scene. And so forth and so on.

There are, in addition, myriad studies and essays that examine the links between the remembering self and the remembered self. These studies are helping us to build steadily and surely a complex picture of a hugely complex set of processes. But what can they tell us about the everyday experiences of recalling the past? When put together, these works offer up a tripartite picture of how remembered self and current self connect: memories of the past that support and illustrate a current self-presentation, memories that create a kind of explanation or continuity with the current self, and memories of the past to create a new self. Let us look at each of these in turn.

## The memory as template

In his poem "All Our Yesterdays," Jorge Luis Borges reminds us that there are many memories of self in the past one might choose to think of or share with others:

> I need to know who lays claim to my past.
> Who, of all those I was? The Geneva boy
> Who learned some Latin hexameters with joy,
> Lines that the year and decades have erased?
> That child who searched his father's library for
> Exact details, the round-cheeked cherub storms
> Of the old maps, or else the savage forms
> That are the panther and the jaguar?
> Or the one who opened a door and looked upon
> A man as he lay drawing his last breath,
> Leaving forever, and kissed in the white dawn
> The face that stiffens away, the face in death?
> I am those that are no more. For no good reason
> I am, in the evening sun, those vanished persons.

Borges reminds us that there are many memories of self in the past that one might choose to think of or share with others. What makes us recall a certain episode, and more to the point, why do certain episodes become staples of our internal autobiography? In Judith Sensibar's examination of the life and work of William Faulkner, she claims that his early experiences of a racist culture (the deep South during the early twentieth century) and his unsatisfying relationships with a black mammy and a white mother provided powerful themes for much of his adult writing. In this sense, she claims, Faulkner's autobiography can be unearthed from his fiction. She cites a memory he describes of himself at age 3, being carried by his black mammy.

> I will be awfully glad to see Vanneye again. The last time I remember seeing her was when I was 3, I suppose. I had gone to spend the night with Aunt Willie (in Ripley) and I was suddenly taken with one of those spells of loneliness and nameless sorrow that children suffer, for what or because of what they do not know. And Vanneye and Natalie brought me home, with a kerosene lamp. I remember how Vanneye's hair looked in the light — like honey. Vanneye was impersonal; quite aloof: she was holding the lamp. Natalie was quick and dark. She was touching me. She must have carried me.

Sensibar claims that this memory crystallizes Faulkner's sense of conflict between a beloved black mother, one whom he feels genuinely intimate with but cannot ultimately have, and a distant, aloof white mother. She argues that the memory is a screen memory and that it captures a theme of his life that became a theme of his fiction.

The idea of a screen memory is an alluring one. Freud coined the phrase to describe a memory that is a cover-up for a more dangerous, id-governed memory. Screen memories tend to be safe, moderately bland, and, according to Freud, always conceal some deeper material. Sensibar suggests that a screen memory also serves to condense into scenario form the themes and issues that may have rambled through and pervaded life. How do we know Faulkner's memory is not a real memory? How do we know he didn't create it as a justification of the theme of racial tension in his books? It turns out that Faulkner first put this screen memory into writing soon after his first work of fiction was published. It may be that he recalled this scene to make sense of his fiction. That doesn't make the memory untrue; it just helps explain how and why he recalled the scene when he did. As a single event, even if it happened just as Faulkner recalls, it is doubtful it caused him to have a lifelong conflict about maternal figures and race. It is likely that the memory stands for a series of events that represent a conflict running through Faulkner's life. It is also possible that as these themes began to emerge in his published writing, memories such as the one just described became salient to him as a way of explaining the themes in his fiction. Faulkner's memory is a good example of the way in which context determines what is recalled, and the way in which one's particular situation (writing novels in this case) causes one to forge particular links between past and present.

I have been describing the way in which a particular scene from the past serves to illuminate or explain a current aspect of the self. But is there any order or significance to the kinds of things we focus on in our recollections? In Sensibar's analysis of Faulkner's screen memory she notes the sense of disturbing illogic within the memory. She points out that on first reading it one finds a semblance of narrative coherence. Upon closer inspection the memory reveals a sense of unresolved and unexplained threads. In this sense, the order—or apparent disorder, as the case may be—provides a guide to interpretation. What is left out and what is put in, and the sense generated from the sequence of details and events, tell a lot not only about what happened in a person's life but what those memories mean to the person.

Many of an adult's most vivid or important memories of childhood convey that quality of disturbance, something unexplained, or unresolved. That sense of irresolution may fuel your need to recall it. As we develop and discover the sense-making power of the past, we may focus more and more on those memories that capture puzzles or ambiguities—just the things that we need to figure out who we are.

I have always recalled the dismal time I had when, at age 5, I had my tonsils taken out. I recall being told it would be fun, that I would get lots of candy and ice cream to eat. I recall waking up in the hospital, the night before the surgery, and playing a game of Space Bug with my mother, who stayed with me. I recall how wretched I felt when I came out of surgery, how shocked I was by the unexpected pain in my throat. And I recall the loving concern with which my divorced parents let me choose which of them should drive me to my home 2 hours away on Long Island. I also recall the misery I felt at having chosen my father, how much I really wanted my mother, but how carefully I acted like I was glad I had asked my father. Finally, I recall the stop we made at his mother's house so that I could sample her wonderful melon balls, but my throat hurt too much to enjoy them, and I was too miserable wishing that I was with my mother to enjoy anything.

What is more interesting than this sort of narrative that I have dredged up now and then to myself, and to others, when talking about tonsillectomies, childhood hospital stays, the game of Space Bug, is how and when the memory became truly meaningful and reconnected. Just a few years ago I was faced with a difficult job decision. My ambivalence and sense of total paralysis in the face of this decision were bewildering. In an effort to reach some clarity, I took a long, hot bath. I lay there tormenting myself about why a decision in which both options seemed so good would be so incapacitating to me. And that is the moment when I recalled the tonsillectomy and understood why I had continued to recall it. Because what was really meaningful about the memory was that I had been so overwhelmed by having to choose between my mother and my father. Two seemingly good choices.

And I had chosen the parent I thought I should choose—the one I didn't live with, the one I felt more ambivalent about, the one who might be hurt if I didn't choose him. Even though I really wanted to go with the other parent. Having made the "good" choice, I regretted it terribly. That was what the memory really meant. The memory was always meaningful, always had a narrative form that gave it several points of entry, or connection. But any of these points of entry had to be "taken" for the memory to be used or experienced in any real sense. Memories can tell you what happened, but they feel so potent and powerful because they explain who you are. I knew all along what happened when I had my tonsils out, but when I realized how the memory illuminated who I am, a whole other level of meaning was added, not only to my present but to my past. And in discovering the real meaning of the memory, the core or locus of the event shifted for me. The operation itself no longer seemed to be at the center of the memory. The question of emphasis, so important in narrative studies, turns out to be central to understanding memory as well. Subtleties such as emphasis and tone are as important for understanding a construction of the past as are the grosser elements, such as the inclusion or exclusion of crucial details.

This example also makes clear that a template memory—a memory that stands for a larger, more diffuse meaning of theme in a person's life—can be discovered unwittingly, or used deliberately. To begin with, I wasn't seeking out a story that would explain my difficulty making decisions. However, a somewhat self-reflective personality, combined with a moment that demanded self-understanding, catapulted me into the memory. Having uncovered the meaning of the memory and constructed it as a template for a theme in my life, I will now refer to it in a much quicker, neater fashion when trying to explain to myself or others the theme of indecision in my life. This suggests that the line from unbidden memory, to insight, to deliberate use is more fluid than one might think.

## The memory of everyday life

In recent years with all the attention to and concern about the reality of repressed memories, there has been an understandable focus on the remembering and repressing of traumatic events. But for most people, most of the time, the personal past is not made of disastrous events, but rather a weaving together of humdrum but revealing details and activities, with major events that are significant more for their subjective impact than for their external drama.

Ask people to recount their life story and they will talk about the setting of their early life (place, family structure, time in history) and they will describe their development in terms of internal turning points—experiences that marked changes in perspective, understanding, or their sense of self in relation to the world. The architect Stanford White's great-granddaughter recalls her grandmother remembering one such emotionally charged moment of her young adulthood, the time she had planned a party for her parents:

> Once, she had arranged a dinner in honor of her parents, and at the last minute, just before the guests were to arrive, Daisy and Winty [her parents] swept down the stairs in evening clothes and told Laura that they had other plans, that she was on her own with her fancy guests. This was supposed to be a joke, and my grandmother always told it that way. Her parents had tossed her a challenge—a challenge that she roundly deserved for having such grandiose ideas. Yet she also admitted that, left on her own, she had been terrified and humiliated. And then Stanford [her soon to be father-in-law] arrived. He summed up what had happened, took over the role of host, and made the evening a success. Even when she told this story in old age, my grandmother was grateful to Stanford for saving her. She laughed, but her feelings— gasping fear, followed by relief—were still fresh.

Many people express who they are by conveying the details of their life; those details are usually what make an autobiography interesting. Those little scenes, rather than the grand events, are what capture for teller and listener alike the specificity, uniqueness, and significance of the person's life. It is the experience of lives we want to know about more than the facts of the life. A student in my course on autobiography announced on the first day of class that she didn't appreciate the work of psychologists. In discussing why some details of early life are recalled and others forgotten, she insisted that there was no particular significance to which things are remembered and which are not. "For instance," she said, "I have this vivid recollection of sitting in the cafeteria in kindergarten and smelling the milk from those little milk containers. That has absolutely no importance or meaning in my life. I don't even like milk. In fact, I cannot stand it. It's pure chance that that is the detail I recall." I said nothing to this, but went on discussing the ideas of Sigmund Freud, Donald Spence, Roy Schafer, and Jefferson Singer and Peter Salovey (all of whom discuss the significance of seemingly insignificant details from the past). A week or so later, this is what appeared in her response journal for the course: "Perhaps there is some meaning to my memory of milk. I am adopted, you know. So I was never nursed. I really loathe the smell of milk. Perhaps my memory has something to do with my preoccupation about being separated from my mother at birth."

This woman discovered the meaning of a seemingly random piece of her past in the context of learning about the psychology of memory. It is the rule rather than the exception for people to recall bits of their past without knowing what the meaning of the bit holds. The author Binjamin Wilkomirski, in attempting to convey the world through the eyes of a 3-year-old, says, "I have some shreds of memory still, like a brief flash of light, but their meaning is much less clear." In other words, the rememberer may recall the past but experience a sense of blankness regarding the meaning or import of the recollection.

When authors attempt not to add any layer of detail or cohesion that was not part of the original memory, they try to separate the stored image from the significance that image may hold for them or for their account. These two examples illustrate two related points: that memories can be recalled at one time and the meaning of the memory discovered at another time. For the student in my autobiography class, the recollection felt at first like an unexplained object from the past, and only later took on a meaning and coherence with respect to other memories and to their present identities. In addition, the reasons one might have for recalling a piece of the past, in other words, the orientation one takes toward the past, will influence one's ability to find. the meaning. Often one has to need or want to know the meaning of the past in order to find out what it is. Coming up with a template memory is partly a matter or recollection and partly a matter of orientation toward the past. Why are you recalling, and who are you telling?

In her memoir, *The Road from Coorain*, Jill Ker Conway describes her childhood in an extremely isolated region of Australia. What makes the early part of the book so compelling are the details of such a life—how a young girl spent her days in the outback. Her choice of the details to describe reflects her reason for telling her life story. She wants to show how such a past might lead to a life as an American scholar and an academic. In another poignant memoir, *Lost in Translation*, the writer Eva Hoffman describes what it was like to emigrate from Poland to Canada in the middle of the twentieth century. The most evocative and important parts of the book are her descriptions of what it was like to begin living in a new language:

> Every day I learn new words, new expressions. I pick them up from school exercises, from conversations, from the books I take out of Vancouver's well-lit, cheerful public library. There are some turns of phrase to which I develop strange allergies. "You're welcome," for example, strikes me as a gaucherie, and I can hardly bring myself to say it—I suppose because it implies that there 's something to be thanked for, which in Polish would be impolite. . . . Then there are words to which I take an equally irrational liking, for their sound, or just because I'm pleased to have deduced their meaning. Mainly they're words I learn from books, like "enigmatic" or "insolent"— words that have only a literary value, that exist only as signs on the page.

Often what makes an autobiography compelling is not the dramatic event but the dramatic insight, the intense view the author has of a seemingly prosaic event. Sharon Olds captures this breathtakingly in her poem about lisping as a child, "The Lisp." The poem recounts how, as a child, Olds was made to feel that her talk was unwelcome. But on Sunday mornings at the breakfast table they would invite her to say "Sharon swallows sausages" because it amused them to hear her lisp. A tiny invitation, the kind that happens every day in every household, is given sharp clarity and conveys a wellspring of personal meaning. No murders, incest, wars, or moments of genius here. Just talk at the breakfast table. But it is these kinds of moments that make up a life.

### Memory as chronology: The search for continuity

In her short story "A Conversation with My Father," Grace Paley tells of how her father had asked her to write a simple story, the kind in which she would describe real people and what they do:

> I *would* like to try to tell such a story, if he means the kind that begins: "there was a woman . . . " followed by a plot, the absolute line between two points which I've always despised. Not for literary reasons, but because it takes all hope away. Everyone, real or invented, deserves the open destiny of life.

People have a powerful drive to experience themselves as continuous across space and time. Because of this there is a strong impulse to make an explanatory line from one moment and event in one's life to another. While many have claimed that this drive is the central force behind all memory and narrative, it has a specific manifestation in the urge to tell the life story as a series of connected events. When people connect life events, they are likely, either deliberately or unconsciously, to weave together a significant chronology—a line of connection that reveals meaning about their life. Some might argue that chronology is what distinguishes autobiography from memoir. Gore Vidal and others have suggested that a memoir can be incomplete, nonchronological, and give a sense of your memories, while an autobiography must document the life lived over time. As a literary distinction this may be useful. But from a psychological perspective, it may be more interesting to ask why, or under what circumstances, people try to make some kind of continuity or link between events in their lives. For some, it is not the events themselves that reveal or contribute to a sense of self, but the connections between events that point to the self. Many writers have described this process wonderfully.

Russell Baker gets right to the heart of this matter in his essay on writing his own memoir. He argues that what is accurate is not necessarily honest. Baker describes the process of trying to write his own life story, *An American Boyhood*. He began by dutifully interviewing his vast family of siblings and aunts, uncles, and cousins. He then took these copious transcripts and notes and carefully crafted the information into a portrait of the early years of his life. He claims that what he ended up with was deadly boring, completely correct, and ultimately dishonest.

In rereading his manuscript he realized that he had to go back and lose all that information and instead tell the *story* of his childhood. In other words, rather than collecting accurate information and organizing it to match the objective unfolding of events (present the facts in chronological order), he had to discover the theme of his childhood. The theme was the relationship between a mother and her son (him). For Baker, adherence to the external "truth" of events had concealed rather than revealed the meaning of his early life. Once he identified this theme and expressed the theme as it was manifested through various events, characters, and details that occurred over time, and in place, he had a story and an honest, if inaccurate, memoir.

His description of the process of writing the story of his childhood illuminates a powerful psychological idea: chronological memory serves one's self-concept. If one doesn't discover the self in a chronology, it isn't really autobiographical memory. In other words, a strictly accurate and objectively verifiable account of what happened when doesn't necessarily say much to rememberer or listener. The chronology serves the purpose of creating meaning as well as continuity in a life story. Often it is the distortions in chronology (deliberate or unconscious) that reveal the true meaning of what happened. Several writers have pointed out that a chronology is necessarily selective. What gets selected has to do with the point, or in Baker's terms, the story that the rememberer is trying to construct.

Annie Dillard, in her reflections on writing her memoirs, distinguishes between an autobiography and a memoir. She argues, like others before and after her, that an autobiography is a record of where and when, and a memoir focuses on specific experiences. Writing a memoir requires a tighter focus on a smaller area. Perhaps the lens used in memoirs is more obviously distorted than that used for autobiography. Certainly it seems that literary critics hold memoirs to a different set of truth criteria than they do autobiographies. The distinction when made by an author or a critic points to two ways of using the past to connect to the present.

Dillard says that the main decisions the memoirist must make are what to put in and what to leave out. This is essentially what all rememberers must decide, whether they make these choices deliberately or unconsciously. The difference, or one of the differences, between Dillard and the nonwriter thinking about a past event is that nonwriters usually don't exert much deliberate control over what goes into the memory and what is left out. But these two deciding principles are at work nonetheless. Instead of the conscious mind deciding what to put in and what to leave out, specific characteristics of personalities and situations make these decisions. For instance, if one is looking to explain the origins of one's creative work, as many writers do, the remembered events will all circle around that theme. The lines between those events will create a path toward adult artistry. In her memoir *The Road from Coorain,* Jill Ker Conway wants to show us how a child growing up in a sexist society in the Australian outback could become a leading academic. The events, vivid and revealing on their own, are linked together in such a way that they bring reader and writer to the inevitable end point: the writer's academic success as an adult. Annie Dillard says that she decided what to put in and what to leave out on the basis of what she thought the real story was: the originality and liveliness of her childhood, and the relationship between her inner mental life and the life of the American landscape. Story came first, what to leave in and what to take out came second. This parallels Jerome Bruner's claim that narrative drives memory rather than the other way around.

The urge to find significance in past events coincides with the urge to find consistency in one's self-concept. These in tandem drive the chronology that most people create in their life story.

## Creating lives: Real or imagined

When does selection and editing lead to the creation of fiction? Where does constructing meaning turn into making things up? Everyone, to some extent, embellishes, edits, streamlines, and otherwise colors both templates and chronologies so that they illuminate the self in the present context. But where, or what, is the boundary between creative recollection and fiction that draws on memory?

The novelist Nadine Gordimer has written about what it means to create a fictive life in a novel or short story. And each writer in his or her own way argues for the idea that writers use experiences, people, and objects to express thoughts and perceptions. In her essay "Adam's Rib," Nadine Gordimer writes about using people and people's lives as sources for her fictional characters. She says that it is absurd for people to ask if so and so is really so and so. No character in a book can simply be a real person. She argues that every fictional character has sparks and pieces from those the writer has encountered. She refers to Primo Levi's idea of a "metamir," a mirror that reflects back the looker's perceptions rather than the physical reality.

Gordimer describes her singular experience of creating a character that did borrow from a real person she knew. She even took part of a real speech this real person made and included it as part of her fictional character's speech. After writing the book, she sent a copy of the manuscript to the real man's daughter (a political prisoner in South Africa, he had died by the time she wrote the book). She sent it so that the daughter wouldn't be upset that she had pried into the family members' lives. Gordimer was worried that the daughter might be particularly infuriated at all the imagined parts that were not at all about the real man's real life or family, but would be taken to be so because of the partial resemblance of the character to the man.

One day the daughter came to visit Gordimer, carrying the copy of manuscript. And after they had chatted a little while, during a pause in the conversation, the daughter pointed to the manuscript and said, "This was our life." Gordimer says of that statement:

> For she was not speaking of verisimilitude, she was not matching mug shots, she knew that facts, events, sequences were not so; she was conceding that while no one can have total access to the lives of others—not even through means of the analyst's casebook, the biographer's research, the subjectively composed revelations of diaries and letters—by contrast, on her or his vision the novelist may receive, from the ethos those lives give off, a vapor of the truth condensed, in which, a finger tracing upon a window pane, the story may be written.

The synthesizing, transforming act of writing fiction may simply be a more deliberate and thus more licensed version of what we all do when we remember. We create our own metamirs through our autobiographical memory. In a sense, most autobiographical memories zero in on moments of interaction (or combustion) between the outer world and the inner world. Our memories of the personal past seem to capture the quality of our relations to others, or in some cases the lack of that relation. To the extent that both templates and chronologies serve to express our subjectivity and the connections between the inner and outer, public and private, worlds, then our autobiographical memories are constantly an effort to communicate to ourselves and others our subjective experience. When we focus on the contexts in which memories are constructed, it helps us to differentiate between situations in which one can, in William Zinsser's term, invent the truth, and situations in which such invention becomes a breach of the rules of the exchange of memories; in which condensed truth becomes outright fabrication. In other words, invention in one context of remembering is lying in another. Sometimes people just lie about their past, and when we find out we are shocked and disapproving. There are several recent cases of this that illustrate the boundary between creative everyday distortion and lying.

## Broyard: Meaningful omissions

In his profile of the late book critic Anatole Broyard, Henry Louis Gates brings up several riveting questions about the nature of truth and disclosure in the context of describing one's life. Broyard, who was a well-known book critic for the *New York Times* during the 1960s, a visible member of the New York literary crowd, and quite a ladies' man was also, as it turns out, of black heritage, though his skin color and physical features made it easy for him to pass as white. The reason this is at all interesting is because, for the most part, Broyard kept his racial heritage a secret from his friends, employers, and colleagues. He even kept it secret from his children. I use the term "racial heritage" rather than "racial identity," because clearly Broyard did identify himself, for himself, as black. To the extent that your identity has to do with your thoughts and feelings, and rests on a construction of self rather than historical or biological facts, blackness was not a part of Broyard's identity, just a part of his history.

Broyard's presentation of his life offers an intriguing example of an irrefutable fact being suppressed. There is nothing subjective or iffy about the thing in his past he chose to suppress and thus revise. One can interpret why or how he did it, but that he did it is not up for interpretation. Gates argues that Broyard didn't actually lie and say he had white parents. Rather, he said little or nothing about his parents. In his descriptions of his personal history he circled around their blackness (he said he came from a poor family or a southern family but not a Negro family).

Though Gates is correct that Broyard didn't make false statements, his dissembling constitutes a powerful form of lying, though the lie isn't actually contained in any one autobiographical text. Rather, the effect of what is said creates a lie. The listener or reader is left with an erroneous impression of what is true. No one thing Broyard is known to have said or written was a lie. But when someone heard the things he did say about his family, he or she was left with the impression that Broyard was from a white family. This demonstrates the idea that what you leave out of your autobiography is just as important as what you put in. In Henry James's complicated novel, *Wings of the Dove,* Kate Croy is a woman immersed in the moral struggle between openness and deception. She clearly thinks that lying is beneath her, yet feels forced by circumstance to deceive people right and left. In one classic example, she is at a museum, secretly meeting her lover. When she accidentally meets her friend Millie (Kate has strong reasons for wanting to deceive Millie about the affair, and an equally strong motivation to be intimate with Millie), she says quickly to Millie, "I'm here with Merton Densher." She tells the absolute truth. But her intention is to deceive. By disclosing that she and Densher are together, Kate creates the impression that the meeting is meaningless, and that she has nothing to hide. Intention and what is left out create the lie.

All of us leave things out of our life story. In fact, in a literal sense, much more gets left out than put in, in anyone's life story. Broyard's case raises the question of which omissions or nondisclosures matter and which don't. Broyard didn't set out to document his life, though it was documented to some extent through his extensive writings. But the life that emerges across one's stories and essays is not exactly the same as an autobiography or a memoir. On the other hand, his writings do make reference to his life and his past and in that sense he creates a false past in his texts. (I am agnostic in this context with regard to the morality of lying about one's past. In Chapters 5 and 6, the motivations for deliberate omissions and distortions will be discussed at greater length.) But Broyard also told and lied about his life in casual conversations.

One constantly omits details when recounting past events. Most omissions are simply cognitively efficient, or economical. For instance, when describing going out to a restaurant, you leave out all the details that you assume others already know. You walked in and were seated. You were handed menus. You read the menus. Depending on the audience you might leave out other items as well, knowing that the listener already knows those things. Other details you leave out because you feel they are not pertinent to your story (what you wore, what you ate, who else was in the restaurant, what the waitress was like, what you talked about).

Finally, there are what I call motivated omissions: things you don't want your listener to know. And these too differ in terms of whether you think they matter or not. For instance, you might not want someone to know that you spent over $100 on the dinner. But you make a decision that it doesn't really matter whether someone knows that or not, so you feel okay about not mentioning it. It's the "what she doesn't know won't hurt her" rationale. On the other hand, there are times when you omit information from a recollection or recounting, and know it does matter, but you choose not to disclose anyway. For instance, imagine that I told a secret of yours at dinner. And that it really might affect you to have my dinner companion know. But I don't want you to be mad at me, so I don't tell you it happened.

The point here is that there are three levels of omission in the ordinary course of recalling the past: two that have little bearing on the self and one that has a great deal to do with the self. The first two have to do with cognitive and social economy—leaving out what doesn't matter or what is assumed to be known. The third kind has to do with leaving out pieces that conflict with the self you are presenting, even if that self is patently made up.

An interesting question one can ask about any nondisclosure, omission, or lie about the past is whom it affects, and whether it matters. When does one's memory or autobiography raise moral questions? In Broyard's case, the disturbing fact is that it does matter whether someone is black or not. It shouldn't, but the fact that it does is related to the fact that he suppressed it. If it didn't matter, his omitting it wouldn't matter. It would be like failing to tell you his mother had big feet or his father played golf. And ironically one's race is quite memorable, proof of its saliency in human interactions (one never forgets the race or sex of someone one's met, no matter what else might be forgotten).

It's Broyard's secret that makes his life more interesting to read about. We always want to know the thing people don't want us to know, which is in itself an interesting paradox. Why is it that we want to know what others don't want us to know? Because we assume if they don't want us to know it, it must be interesting, revealing, important in some way. This, and the fact that information is itself a source of power and pleasure. When you know about someone's life you have a kind of currency toward that person and in reference to him or her.

Imagine a group of friends sitting around talking about an absent but mutual acquaintance. Someone says, "I just found out that Aaron has a twin brother." Imagine the satisfaction of being the one in the room to say, "Oh yes. I've known that for years." Beyond the obvious, that knowledge about a person's life suggests intimacy, the more of someone's autobiography you know the more power you have with that person and in regard to that person.

An interesting question raised by the case of Broyard is whether we commonly disclose different life stories in different settings. I have tried to suggest up until now that the setting you are in, and the reason you are talking about your past, will have a huge effect on what you say. Conversely, it is reasonable and psychologically compelling to argue that over time the settings and motivations for telling your life story have a deep and substantive influence on what your life story is. I would guess that the issue of race became the pivot, if not the theme, of Anatole Broyard's inner life story, and that that was dictated as much by the settings in which he was called up to talk about his past as it was by any stable internal feature of his identity.

## Who is the remembered self?

The writer Verlyn Klinkenborg is recalling his early years as a student at Berkeley. Because he is a writer, he is also watching himself recall, and thinking about what it means. He says,

> Augustine has been talking about the nature of memory. "All this goes on inside of me," Augustine says, "in the vast cloisters of my memory. In it are the sky, the earth, and the sea, ready at my summons. . . . In it I meet myself as well." Like Augustine, I also find the sky, the earth, and the sea, ready at my summons. But when I meet myself in memory I'm surprised at how insubstantial I seem, as if I were meeting the memory of a person who is composed only of memories. That's how it truly is, I supposed. What order I detect in that person, in that memory of memories, is the effect of perspective, of lines converging.

The self created through memories is constantly interacting with the self one's memory creates. And this complex and wildly imaginative process is always at the beck and call of the people for whom one is remembering. The remembering self is a self that exerts great influence over what is recalled. That self is simultaneously changed by the memories that are recalled. Now imagine this dynamic mutual influence modulated and shaped by people the remembering self is with, and whatever purposes memory is being put to. One can only imagine a highly volatile chemical interaction between two substances that not only influence one another but do so in different ways, depending on the container they are in and the specific way in which they are mixed.

CHAPTER FIVE
# REMEMBERING IN PRINT

A confessional passage has probably never been written that didn't stink a little bit of the writer's pride in having given up his pride. The thing to listen for, every time, with a public confessor, is what he's *not* confessing to. At a certain period of his life (usually, grievous to say, a *successful* period), a man may suddenly feel it Within His Power to confess that he cheated on his final exams at college, he may even choose to reveal that between the ages of twenty-two and twenty-four he was sexually impotent, but these gallant confessions in themselves are no guarantee that we'll find out whether he once got piqued at his pet hamster and stepped on its head.

—J. D. Salinger

## How we begin: Developmental origins of autobiography

A 3-year-old is asked to tell all about his life. His mother has brought into school two photographs: one showing him as a newborn, the second taken when he was about $2\frac{1}{2}$. The teacher has pasted each picture on a piece of paper, stapled the pieces together, and has told him he is making a book about his life. She asks him what she should write about to go under the picture of him as a newborn baby. He says:

> My mom carried me. Julio, Tina's boy, held me. I cried. Because my mom left me at home without her, with the cat and the dog. My mom made me a cake with frosting, with frosted dolphins. I ate chicken. I swallowed it because I didn't have any teeth.

They turn to the next photo, and again the teacher asks the little boy what she should write to go with the photograph. He dictates,

> I like to watch "Spiderman." I watch it with Daniel and Tim. I like to play that I pretend I'm going to Disney World. You know, Darth Vader has a light saber sword. Well, I pretend I see that at Disney World. I let Mommy sleep in her own bed now, since I sleep in Daniel's bed with Daniel. Daddy sleeps up in Mommy's bed.

This 3-year-old, Barrett, has just taken his first stab at writing an autobiography. Though much has been made—by me among others—of the natural proclivity humans have for narrating their life, ordering experiences into story forms, and sharing life stories with others, we don't start out life with an inclination to write an autobiography. There are powerful continuities between personal reminiscing and autobiographical writing, and the two processes influence one another. Nevertheless, the two are distinct activities. While children as young as 18 months of age can recall an incident from their past, there is a long and multifaceted journey from that first reference to the past to the moment of sitting down to write one's memoirs. What are the lines of connections between recalling a moment in one's past and writing a book about one's life? What makes a person write an autobiography? What kind of remembering is involved in such a work? After all, autobiographical writing constitutes yet another social context (in addition to conversations among parents and children, lovers, and friends, and in therapy and the courtroom) in which memories are created, exchanged, and internalized.

Barrett does a number of interesting and revealing things in his first autobiographical work. In each case his omissions, revelations, and style hint at the important questions autobiography poses for the student of memory.

In order to see what might be the precursors to adult autobiography, it is worth noting what distinguishes Barrett's task and his approach to the task from any adult, writer or otherwise, who might try his or her hand at writing about the past. Barrett didn't arrive at school thinking he would like to tell his life story in writing. He has little or no notion of what a life story is, and only an emerging awareness of the printed word. Barrett offered information about himself to fulfill a task. He is trying to oblige his teacher and fill in an idea she has outlined: tell your life story. Even the pictures that supplied the visual framework of the task, and possibly served as cues or stimuli for what Barrett said, were chosen not by him but by his mother. Adults often frame what children say and do. They create a mental and linguistic foundation on which children can build new skills. In this case Barrett's mother and teacher lead him by the hand, as it were, into an activity that he is not yet ready to initiate, understand fully, or master, but for which he has some component information and abilities and a natural inclination to learn. Mother and teacher collude to create a framework from which Barrett can begin learning how to use his past. By choosing the pictures and asking him to talk about what his life is, they are both enabling him to reminisce and shaping his notion of both the structure and function of autobiography.

There are several characteristics to his fledgling autobiography that are instructive and hint at the problems of the adult autobiographer. Barrett understands that he is being asked to talk about his origins, his early life. This is why he begins by talking about being carried. He chooses what might or might not be an incidental feature of his early dependence on adults, a time when an acquaintance carried him around. But many great autobiographies contain memories that are specific and seem idiosyncratic, yet reflect larger themes. Often great writers' detailed images from the past do not seem to be representative of life epochs in any direct or obvious way. Like Barrett, they choose small, clear details that in some way or another stand out. Woolf's begins with a patch of flowered fabric, Tolstoy's with a fly over his bed.

Barrett tries to reveal how different he was as a baby—lacking teeth and unable to chew. And unwittingly or not, he focuses in on an emotionally charged aspect of his early life—his fears and sense of being left by his mother. By setting this after talking about a special cake she made him (one she denies ever having made), his first autobiographical piece could be interpreted in much the same way as Nabokov's writing about his mother: her power to please, lavish, and abandon. And, as with the autobiographies of adult writers, his portrayal is open to interpretation.

The second page of his autobiography is more chaotic and possibly less meaningful. It is a description of him in the present, what he likes to do. What does come across, again, is his sense of priority. We know what is important to him—playing with Daniel and Tim (his brothers) and pretending. These would seem to be the appropriate predominating themes for a child of 3. So again, unwittingly, even artlessly, Barrett at age 3 has followed a rule of autobiographical narrative: use external life information to reveal who you really are.

And that brings us to the clincher of Barrett's short autobiography, his revealing end. He tells us he now lets Mommy sleep with Daddy, and he has moved out of their bed. How better to describe a central theme in the life of a 3-year-old boy? He has given his mother back to his father and is now sleeping with his brother, a true ally. In sum, Barrett has done several things not unlike what the adult autobiographer does: he has told about his origins, revealed what is important not only in his outer life, but more interesting, his inner life, and described an important turning point (moving from his parents' bed to his brother's bed).

It is clear that the self as a construction and a work of art begins early, at least for some children. But people don't just happen on the process of making themselves through telling their life story. It is an intrinsic part of being human to draw on one's past, both implicitly and explicitly, and to experience events in a story form. However, it is not an inevitable part of being human to write one's autobiography. Instead, we are brought into the activity, its requirements and its uses, through the adults around us and the artifacts they expose us to and invite us to create. Age 3 is pretty young to begin thinking about one's life as a story that can be told and shared with others, but it is not too young to be introduced to samples of autobiography. Barrett (like most children in our culture) will encounter myriad autobiographies, references to autobiographical information, uses of autobiography, and autobiographical contexts and tasks by the time he is 21. Children from 18 months to 3 years hear and are asked to participate in reminiscing with their parents. Research has shown that how much reminiscing a child is exposed to varies as a function of both cultural values and family style of interaction. Children in school are encouraged to talk about their life story in bits and pieces, in show and tell, in writing assignments, and in conversations with teachers. As young friends spend more time talking instead of playing with one another, they also begin talking more and more with one another about their lives. In one study I conducted, 3-year-olds barely responded to one another's offerings of life information. But 5-year-olds were talking quite extensively about what kinds of houses they lived in, what their family members do and say, and what adventures (both good and bad) they have had outside of the school setting. While few of us ever come to actually write down our whole life story, the autobiography as a form of representing life is ubiquitous in our culture. Even though so few of us actually write our own in a full-fledged form, we all use autobiographies, our own and those we read, to find order in our lives and to gain understanding about ourselves and the social world around us.

A child of 3 would almost certainly not come up with an autobiography if he weren't asked, coaxed, and helped to form one. The tendency of most adults to narrate their lives while living them appears effortless and spontaneous. Much has been made in recent years of the pervasiveness of the inner life story. Clinical and cognitive psychologists have explored the ways in which people mentally file things away as personal remembrances and draw on those memories in order to construct a personal history. References to it in literary criticism, psychology, and common parlance would suggest that the autobiography is ubiquitous. But the impulse to communicate one's whole life as a single coherent story only comes with mental growth and acculturation. There are several illuminating reasons why children don't typically offer up autobiographies and can't even do it "properly" when so asked.

First of all, children under the age of 5 are still fairly rooted in the here and now. While interested in hearing about their past, they don't spend much time reflecting on what their lives mean, on how they got to where they are, or on what their past can tell them about their current self. And these, after all, are generally the motivations for private autobiographical thinking. On the other hand, the more social or public motivations for recalling one's past are also not operative for most young children most of the time. It is only very recently, and still rarely the case, that children are called upon as witnesses to their own past. Therapy for young children rarely involves asking them to narrate their brief lives. Instead, the story of their life is interpreted from their play. And the use of the past as a way of building friendships and intimacy only emerges slowly, in bits and pieces, during the first 7 years of peer interaction.

Children as young as 16 months show special interest in their parents' references to the past. They become attentive, quiet, and responsive when their parents tell them stories about things that they have done, seen, or experienced. Within the first 3 years, many children are able and willing participants in the act of reminiscing.

There lie the seeds of possible autobiographies. But there is a world of difference, psychologically speaking, between referring to or describing something from the past (how I got that cut on my leg) and constructing a life story that tells you who you are and why you are the way you are. What is put into an autobiography, as opposed to personal references to the past, distills forever one's view of the experiencing "I" looking over the varied "me's."

When children as young as 5 are asked to tell their life story, they don't have a template for how to fulfill such a request. They may mix together information about their current situation with odd tidbits about their past. Once started on a moment in the past they may talk extensively about that moment (the time they broke their arm, when they moved to a new town, their first day of kindergarten, etc.), and neglect to describe anything else. The sense of balance that most adults would feel constrained by, the effort to tell about each epoch, to choose clearly important or pivotal moments in life—these narrative requirements are missing from young children's first efforts to create an autobiography.

Also missing, by and large, is the internal motivation that proves to be such a powerful determinant of the adult's autobiography.

It is hard to imagine how anyone would begin to construct a life story, the kind that could or might be written down, without living in a world of people who create such documents. That we live in such a world has two direct effects on the developing child. First, children are highly responsive to the cultural artifacts of their community. If they live in a world of autobiographies, and reference to autobiographies and life story, they are going to notice, emulate, and imitate these spoken and written texts. Moreover, a society that values and uses autobiography as an important source of information is likely to find ways in which to ask children to create their own autobiographies. We do, usually unconsciously, prepare our children to do the things we think adults in our culture should be able to do.

Early on, in many settings, we begin to ask children to compose mini-autobiographies. This happens most typically in school but also may happen in more informal settings. Using these means, we begin asking children to take an autobiographical stance toward their life. This means they view their life as a series of connected incidents in which the links have some meaning. The first event leads to the second event, or a sequence of four events explains why things are as they are. For instance, a child of 5 suggests, in telling his life story, that "the reason I am smart about the woods is because when I was little, my nana took me walking all the time and I learned what everything is called." The self is put at the center of the sequence, and early experiences are seen to shape later characteristics. By 10 years of age, many children seem inclined to describe the past in subjective terms. This reflects their dawning awareness that in our culture it is the subjective past that is most interesting in autobiography. All of these features distinguish the autobiographical stance from other stances one might take in conversation or even in other forms of storytelling.

Once you put your life onto the printed page, it takes on a life of its own. Too little has been written in the recent flood of literature on life story and memory about the differences between telling fragments from the past to another person and actually writing one's life down in words on a page, to be read by strangers. The psychological and social differences between a sentence spoken within a conversation and the effect on writer and reader of a carefully drafted and published text are important. The distance between these two situations invites us to distinguish more carefully between them.

In one study I conducted, children ages 5 to 8 were invited to write their autobiographies with the help of interested college students. In almost all cases, the college student offered to take dictation, and the child was then invited to look over what had been written down in case he or she wanted to add or delete anything from the story. In this way, children were invited to take an autobiographical stance toward their own past experience and to construct something they had never constructed before: a written autobiography. The children varied widely in how they approached the task, though it was clear that all of them noted the special nature of what they were being asked to do.

Some plunged right in, beginning with where and how they were born. These children show implicitly that an autobiography draws as much upon other people's memories of one's life as it does upon one's own memories of that life.

> I was born in 1988 and when I was born my legs were crossed like this.
> [Note: Child crosses legs to demonstrate.]

Other children began with the here and now, and only revealed their life story incidentally through what they said about their present situation.

> I live in the Sally Pierpoint trailer park, S__, Vermont. I build, and I invent stuff. I can read a little books. And, and, I do certain things.

I do . . . lots of stuff. And I have a lot of friends. And I have a mommy and a dad. But my mom stays away from my dad because my dad drinks beer. My mom stays away from my dad because he drinks. That's all.

Unlike the adult author, the children didn't come to this task with a particular reason for constructing their autobiography. Instead, they were simply complying with a request from an appealing adult. But even so, once they began they had to choose an orientation toward the task. There were several interesting differences among the autobiographies we collected. For instance, girls tended to include emotional descriptors (I felt happy, I was mad) and boys didn't. Because of this difference, overall girls' autobiographies drew the reader's attention to the experiencing "I" more than boys' autobiographies did. Most striking, however, was our realization as we collected the data that we were asking them to do something they had never done before: view their life as a text. The differences between genders are one sign that the autobiographical process, while still implicit and untapped, is nevertheless taking shape within the developing child.

## The autobiographical stance

In order to get a psychological picture of what it means to take an autobiographical stance toward one's life, imagine for a moment what was involved in two very different lives and the writers who wrote about them.

Virginia Woolf spent her life immersed in writing and the world of writing. She grew up in a highly literate society. She wrote a great deal about her own life, in diaries, fiction, memoirs, and letters to friends, family, and lovers. Her life is almost exacerbatingly documented. When one looks across the different kinds of writing and sources of documentation about Woolf's life and considers her absolute unwavering commitment to spending time each day writing about herself, it is hard not to come to the conclusion that she lived her life, at least in part, in order to write about it. The lived experience and the written experience exerted more mutual influence on one another than would be the case for most writers (not to mention the rest of us, who, rarely if ever, write about or document our lives).

Now contrast this with the memoir of Kate Simon, *Bronx Primitive*, which convey's a child's view of reality. Events—holidays, illnesses, disasters, visits—seem to burst out of nowhere. Things happen without any explanation. Small details loom large, while whole domains of life fade to the background world of adults. This author doesn't seem to have grown up with the literary sensibility of someone like Woolf. Simon's memories seem to capture the undiluted and unadorned quality of experience.

Or take the memoir *Maus*, by Art Spiegelman. Spiegelman invites, cajoles, and even pressures his father to describe his experiences as a Jew during World War II. Though Spiegelman elicits these memories in order to use them in his cartoon account, his father is talking about things he never thought of telling, much less crafting into art. It is only at the moment of divulging his experiences to his son that these moments of memory begin to take on an order, which in turn expresses narrative meaning. Simon and Spiegelman, though clearly so different, both convey that putting experiences into an explicitly narrative form, with conscious attention to communicative and aesthetic characteristics, came long after the experiences themselves.

These two writers appear to be at the opposite end of the spectrum from Woolf. Woolf seemed to live each moment with one eye on how she would write about it, whereas Simon and Spiegelman are describing a past during which they had little or no thought of writing about it. Indeed, in each of these narratives, it is clear that just living life day to day absorbed their complete attention—Simon because she was a child, and Spiegelman's father because he was living through horrific events that dimmed consciousness and reduced life to immediate crises and impressions. Woolf, on the other hand, experienced daily life with an autobiographical stance: How will I say this? What does it mean? How do I feel? Is this significant? One imagines that these are the kind of questions (conscious or unconscious) that ran through her mind while in conversation, working in the garden, walking, running errands, or in other ways living the life about which she would write.

These represent two very different stances toward the past, toward autobiography as an activity and as a self-making process. The past becomes a different sort of material, and the work of making memories into one's autobiography is very different for different people.

In his book, *Kafka's Other Trial*, Elias Canetti convinces us that Kafka's doomed (and highly literary) love affair with Felice was, in a sense, lived as material and fuel for his writing. In Canetti's analysis of Kafka's letters to Felice, he shows us that Kafka's personal trials fed his work:

> The struggle to obtain this strength which her regular letters bring him does have meaning. It is no empty exchange of letters, no end in itself, no mere self-gratification: it helps his *writing*.

Canetti goes on to claim that the only way to think about a writer's life is in terms of how it affects that writer's writing. Thus any writer who writes about his life is giving us a way of judging his writing. For both rememberer and audience, the life is lived for how it will appear in text.

To write an autobiography is to engage in a self-conscious and deliberate process that draws not only on vast amounts of personal memory but research into one's life, mastery of narrative skills, and an eagerness to communicate a carefully crafted version of oneself to strangers. Though distinct in what it requires, the writing of autobiography has its roots in common, everyday human activities of reminiscing and reporting what one has seen and done. These ordinary, sometimes unexpected, often ephemeral acts of reminiscing and recounting become a whole new activity when employed to construct a written documentation of one's life.

From the moment you sit down to write your autobiography, and usually long before that moment, there are a host of decisions and choices you face that reflect the complex nature of remembering a life. Do you want to document external events and details of your life or are you looking to reveal an inner self? Do you feel that the events are self-evident or that they must be construed in a particular way for the reader to get the impression you want them to get?

The author William Zinsser describes the way in which he used humor to soften the portrait he drew of his mother and sisters in his memoir. In choosing the episodes that captured what seemed important to him about his childhood, he was left with the problem of how his family would feel upon reading the memoir. He had the desire and ability to lighten the tone of these memories through his choice of words and sentences. By crafting the past, we alter it.

Why you want to write your life story guides what you will put into the story and how you will shape it. These choices and motivations surface in ways that reflect and respond to the culture in which you live. Every culture, at any given moment in history, has a point of view about life stories that influences the specific life stories that members of the culture construct.

## The culture of autobiography

We live in a culture that believes that one's experiences are cumulative, continuous, and that there is something to be learned by the author (the self) and the reader (others) by scrutinizing the narrative of one's life. This assumes that events are meaningful, that the experience of those events is even more meaningful, and that there is some fundamental relationship between what you have done and felt and who you are.

None of these assumptions are self-evident. They are all the result of a modern consciousness. Canetti talks brilliantly about why someone interested in an author's fiction would want to know details about the author's life. In explaining the attention he has given to the 5 years during which Kafka wrote to Felice, Canetti writes,

> Is the story of a five-year-long withdrawal so important, one may ask, that it has to be considered in such detail? Interest in a writer can certainly be carried to great lengths. And if the documents are as copious as they are in this case, then it can become irresistibly tempting to know them all and to grasp their internal coherence; the wealth of the documentation only sharpens the critic's appetite. Man considers himself the measure of all things, but he is still almost unknown. His progress in self-knowledge is minimal; every new theory obscures more of him than it illuminates. Only unimpeded concrete inquiry into particular human beings makes gradual advance possible.

Novels written around the turn of the century (those of Henry James, James Joyce, and Thomas Mann come to mind) reflect a turn inward, a focus on the landscape of consciousness, as Bruner puts it, rather than the landscape of action. But the idea that memory provided a literary means of documenting the experienced life first emerged in the work of Augustine, who, in the fourth century, wrote as compellingly about autobiographical memory as anyone since. In *Confessions,* he ignited the genre with his introspections regarding the nature of his memory. His work was the first to articulate the view that one's memories are the text or material of one's life. He framed the idea that a self exists continuously across those memories, a self worth writing about:

> In my memory, too, are all the events that I remember, whether they are things that have happened to me or things that I have heard from others. From the same source I can picture to myself all kinds of different images based either upon my own experience or upon what I find credible because it tallies with my own experience. I can fit them into the general picture of the past; from them I can make a surmise of actions and events and hopes for the future; and I can contemplate them all over again as if they were actually present.

Augustine sets out the framework that continues to inform modern research on the topic: the sense-making capacity of our memory. But it was perhaps Wordsworth, in his autobiographical poem *Prelude,* who first used the lived life as text. He was also one of the early writers to see his internal life as material worth writing about. Central to his work was the notion of the subjective self. His perceptions, feelings, and responses, rather than simply what he did and what happened around him, formed the substance of his poetry. And equally important, he believed that these remembered experiences were the source of his life as an adult writer.

> Fair seed time had my soul, and I grew up
> Fostered alike by beauty and by fear.

The idea that there is continuity to the internal life of a person and significance to the external unfolding of events in a person's life is a modern idea. In his study of nineteenth-century, middle-class Europe, *The Naked Heart,* Peter Gay describes the emergence of a preoccupation with the individual self. This shift in spiritual and epistemological focus created the groundwork for the emergence of the autobiographical genre in literature. It is striking that during a century when the Western bourgoisie gained increasing interest and faith in the objective facts that explain life (biology and neuroscience), they developed a parallel fascination with the internal self and the subjective experience of life.

"My earliest memory is dipped in red." Thus Canetti begins his own memoir. It not only startles the reader with its vividness, it jolts the reader into the awareness that a memoir is about a communication of the images within one person's mind, not a record of what happened. We have seen this preoccupation take on new intensity in the last decade of the twentieth century. As the culture has zeroed in on the lived life as a source of information and insight, advances in neuroscience have demonstrated the complexity of the neurological processes involved in remembering the personal past. Research has shown us that our ability to monitor and reflect on our own remembering processes is part and parcel of the memory apparatus. While images and scenes from the past are available to us because of the way our brains are structured and the way they function, the uses to which we put memory are in part determined by the place and time in which we live. For instance, recent advances have shown that there are certain parts of the brain required for language use but that these physical parts, while necessary, are not sufficient. That is, one could not use language without those parts of the brain, but having those parts does not fully account for language use. In fact, it is what we humans have done with those parts of the brain that has led us to use language where other primates have not. This is a reminder that knowing the physiological bases of a psychological process only gives us one part of the picture. The ways in which we use memory are dependent on factors outside of the physical makeup of our brain.

A friend has gone to his high school reunion, particularly eager to see his old social studies teacher, who had such an important influence on him. When asked how the teaching is going, his old mentor leans forward and says with mock earnestness, "Oh, don't you know? I don't teach social studies anymore. I teach 'Who Am I?'" This anecdote illustrates how Western culture, in particular, at the end of the millennium, has focused on questions of individual identity. That kind of focus has a substantive influence on what we might once have considered to be a completely internal and physically based activity such as remembering.

But it is not simply that we are obsessed with the self, and the internal self at that. We also think that to know a person you have to know the person's life. There is a sense, both formal and informal, in literature and in everyday life, that a person's life story is informative, relevant, and interesting. Take, for instance, Andrew Solomon's account of his struggle with depression. Filled with the vivid details of what it is like to be swept into an acute episode of depression, the account also contains a fair amount of anecdotal and empirical evidence about the causes, treatments, and nature of depression. It is organized completely around the author's personal encounter with depression and makes for gripping reading. But the same article could have been written, and might well have been written 100 years ago, without a life story at its center. This is not a criticism—just a reminder that the current emphasis on the life story is distinctive. This, in turn, reminds us that whatever is intrinsic, "natural," physiologically based about the activity of personal recollection, reminiscing only manifests itself when people exchange personal information and experience with one another. Every autobiographical memory, even a very private one, is thus shaped by the ways in which a community views and uses life-story information.

When adults now sit down to write about their life they do so with the conscious or unconscious awareness that many others have written about their lives, and that readers expect to learn about writers by learning about what the writers have done, seen, and felt. We expect a life to reveal a self. Those of us drawn to reading autobiographies tend to believe that what the person remembers about their past is trust-worthy, valuable, and significant. We usually want to read about the person if they are famous, if we hear that there is something spectacu-lar about their past that is intrinsically interesting, if we love their writing, or if we think there is some link between what they have experienced and our own lives. This expectation guides the reading. We think there is a good reason why they wrote the book in the first place.

This brings us back to the essential question: why would someone write about their life, and how does that motivation shape the process of memory that they engage in to write the autobiography? The im-pulse to write down one's life is a curious one. Rarely is this impulse free from economic and social forces. Most of the people who write their life stories for publication have some expectation that people will want to know about their lives. There are, as already stated, a few rea-sons why someone might expect this. If you are famous (a president, a scientist, an artist, a criminal), people want to know about your life and have some expectation that they will learn how you came to be the way you are through your life experiences. If you have written books that sold well (Nabokov, Roth, and Woolf, for example) then your life is interesting for two reasons: the way you write about it and the possi-bility that it will explain to people how you came to be such a good writer. A second aspect of this is the intrinsic voyeurism of modern life: everyone wants to peer in the window of those who hold our interest. But there are some distinctive motivations for writing autobiographies, and they shape not only the work but also the remembered life.

Writing an autobiography involves thinking of one's whole life. Unlike the remembered life that is told in bits and pieces, told across myriad conversations, the written life has to be thought of as a piece. Of course the writer may work on bits and pieces: some of the time his or her experience of writing a piece is not unlike the usual kind of unbidden memory, where one memory or thought leads unexpectedly to a long forgotten detail or event from the past. Similarly, the writer may discover a theme or meaning to his life that he didn't know was there until he started writing. But the writer, unlike the everyday rememberer, approaches his life as if it were something that could be given structure and put down in words. The writer assumes that he can impose or discover some shape to his life, some way in which his memories, when taken together, make sense, or, more than that, make a story.

In a sparkling and underappreciated memoir, *Nothing to Do but Stay,* Carrie Young describes growing up in the Midwest in the early part of the twentieth century with a mother who was determined that her six children would all get an education, though they lived on an isolated homestead and were poor. With her opening line, Young announces the shape she has discovered in her life: "My mother was wild for education." The story, about a pioneer mother and the childhood of the author and her five siblings, unfolds from that central point—her mother's determination to get them all through school under adverse conditions. We know from that first sentence how to put together the scenes and events we subsequently learn about. Her theme, and the one she sets out for the reader, create cohesion across time and incident.

It is one thing to find the words for a theme or narrative line that gives meaning to one's life experience, yet another to want to communicate that through written words to an audience of unknown readers. The writer must assume an interest on the part of the reader. This is the ticklish part, the part that differs so significantly from speaking about the past. When you speak about the past to friends or relatives you gauge their interest based on your mutual intimacy. You can monitor their reactions as you speak. Their spoken or gestural responses guide what you focus on, omit, or emphasize. When a lawyer or a therapist asks you about the past, they also have a clear and explicit interest and motivation in hearing about you. They too let you know, in subtle or obvious ways, what they want to hear about, what they think is significant, what they accept, and what they reject. The writer, on the other hand, can only predict and imagine the audience's response. In this sense, writing an autobiography is at once a more public and a more solitary kind of remembering. There is great opportunity for revision, for reshaping, for adding and subtracting. Two kinds of forces can direct this revision. One is an impulse to make a better or more readable work, and the other an impulse to tell it like it is and get at the truth. These impulses can as easily conflict with one another as support one another.

One important difference between the kinds of autobiographical remembering we do in conversations and the kinds we do for a written document concerns the level of focus. In everyday remembering you can zero in on one episode either for its intrinsic value and interest or for its connection to some larger theme or sequence of events. But with a written work, each piece is also constantly thought of in terms of its relationship to the whole. If context is central to understanding memory, then it is important to know what constitutes the context of any given type of remembering. In conversations about the past that occur between friends, the interpersonal dynamic of the relationship, the situation in which you are talking, the topic that led you to reminisce, and your internal state at the moment of conversation taken together provide the context in which your memories find shape. In the writing of an autobiography, on the other hand, one's whole life, as it becomes constructed mentally, provides the context for each specific memory. How does this memory connect to that? What overall meaning will that communicate? If I begin here, where will I end? The reconstructed life, rather than the moment of remembering, becomes to a much greater degree the context for recalling the past.

A more vivid picture of the kinds of remembering that take place when people write their lives down emerges from considering specific autobiographies. Each autobiography described in the following pages reveals not only a remembered life but also an underlying motivation that guided the creation of a life story. The five motivations described in the following include persuasion, disguise, transcendence, self-justification, and invitations to peek.

## Persuasion: The three lives of Frederick Douglass

Frederick Douglass started life as a slave. He was born in Maryland in 1818 and attained freedom in 1838. Douglas wrote three separate but overlapping autobiographies—the first in 1845, the next in 1855, and the last in 1881. His self-reported purpose, particularly with the first autobiography, was to show white people in the North that a black person could be educated, literate, and eloquent. What comes through the narrative as well is his determination to show that, contrary to the view held by whites in the mid-1880s, black people had complex experiences, that there was such a thing as a black subjectivity.

His life, and the self that emerges through his account, are defined by his race and the position of a black person in the United States during the nineteenth century. As is so often the case, the shape of his life story is announced in his opening lines:

> I was born in Tuckahoe, new Hillsborough, and about twelve miles from Easton, in Talbot county, Maryland. I have no accurate knowledge of my age, never having seen any authentic record contain it. By far the larger part of the slaves know as little of their ages as horses know of theirs, and it is the wish of most masters within my knowledge to keep their slaves thus ignorant. I do not remember to have ever met a slave who could tell of his birthday, they seldom come nearer to it than planting-time, harvest-time, cherry-time, spring-time, or fall-time. A want of information concerning my own was a source of unhappiness to me even during childhood.

Douglass tells us right up front what is important to him about his life story: where he was born—the American South—turns out to be central, as well as his lack of bearings and orientation about his own origins, due to his slave status, and the pernicious and profound effect of white hatred on the experiences of a black child. He ends this first short segment by telling us that being a slave and the self-concept it led to made him unhappy. The notion that a slave could be unhappy was, no doubt, shocking to many readers of his book and would have been incomprehensible to many of the white people he grew up with, who, no doubt, never did read his book.

Thus his remembered life, though it unfolds in detail over the course of the next 85 pages, is shaped in the first paragraph. Moreover, and this is what seems important to me, telling his life has a purpose: showing what it was like to be a slave and showing that a man of such stature could have come from experiences and origins such as his. He vividly shows the brutal circumstances of his daily life, but more than that, he shows what it *felt* like to be a slave. His emphasis on subjectivity—his evocation of how things sounded and looked to him—gave his described life the power to transform his contemporaneous readers' construal of African-American slaves.

> My new mistress proved to be all she appeared when I first met her at the door, — a woman of the kindest heart and finest feelings. She had never had a slave under her control previously to myself, and prior to her marriage she had been dependent upon her own industry for a living. . . . I was utterly astonished at her goodness. I scarcely knew how to behave towards her. She was entirely unlike any other white woman I had ever seen. I could not approach her as I was accustomed to approach other white ladies. . . . Her face was made of heavenly smiles, and her voice of tranquil music.

There is a constant coupling of facts about slavery, documentation of the external characteristics of Douglass's life, and the experience of being in that life. His narrative slides back and forth between a sort of polemic against slavery and a description of the details of his experience of events. As with many autobiographers, he cannot help commenting on how subsequent events give meaning to earlier events.

> I look upon my departure from Colonel Lloyd's plantation as one of the most interesting events of my life. It is possible, and even quite probably, that but for the mere circumstance of being removed from that plantation to Baltimore, I should have to-day, instead of being here seated by my own table, in the enjoyment of freedom and the happiness of home, writing this Narrative, been confined in the galling chains of slavery.

One of the great things that remembering an experience can give is hindsight, allowing events to make sense in a way they never can as they unfold. In this way memory gives all of us a grasp of our experience that is distinctive from any kind of insight we can have in the moment. Writing does this to an even greater degree because it forces you to decide when to say what, and in what order. Douglass had no control over whose house he went to and to whom he belonged. But he can still wrest meaning from events by placing them in an order that leads him to where he is at the moment of writing. The urge and skill the author has in finding meaning through narrating the past have their origins in the first narratives children create. In a now well-known study of one toddler talking to herself as she went to bed at night, psychologists showed that she too, in an albeit unconscious and rambling way, used her talk about the past to understand it and create meaning from it.

The talking child—or, for that matter, the talking adult—may only stumble upon the meaning made manifest through a narration of the past. But here the writer differs. There is a clear narrative spine to Douglass's writing: how a black slave came to be a free and erudite orator. What remains ambiguous in his tale is how much he attributes his triumph to internal personal characteristics and how much to quirks of fate. What is clear, however, is that he wants to speak for all slaves and in that sense has written a representative memory. His memory speaks for others, though he would never claim to know what each other slave has felt, endured, or thought.

To whom is Douglass speaking? To white readers of the North. To those who doubt the atrocities of the South and doubt the capabilities of the black man. Douglass's autobiography is a polemic aimed at persuading his readers to think differently *about people like him*. To Douglass's mind, his reader is a generalized stand-in for the white people he has encountered when speaking out publicly about the abolition of slavery and about the plight of black people in the South. He is speaking to an internal representation of a body of people. And he is trying at the same time to speak for many, not just for himself.

What is perhaps most intriguing about Douglass as a rememberer is not only the riveting substance of what he says about what was a truly remarkable life, but the fact that he wrote three autobiographies. Why would anyone feel the call to write three versions of his life story?

Douglass's autobiographies vary along two dimensions. First and most obviously they were written at different times, and each represents a different vantage point. But they also speak to different points. The first book, written in 1845, aims to show what the experience of a slave was, and to show that a black man could be an eloquent man. The second autobiography, written in 1855, covers mostly the same material but with more information, greater detail. The pivotal events remain the same, as do their meanings. But where the first is pared down and moves along quite swiftly, outlining the journey from slavery to freedom, the second is more ruminating, focused as much on issues and questions as it is on the chronicle of events. The third, written in 1881, is by far the most polemical and is as much a political position paper as a personal narrative. Each autobiography builds on the core events of Douglass's childhood, and each has somewhat the same message. But as he changed in adulthood, the life story as he wanted it documented and preserved changed. The perspective of the rememberer required a new telling. The idea that each of us has only one story to tell is put to rest by what Douglass has done. He tells the same story three times in three slightly different ways. One doesn't really learn different things about his past when reading the three autobiographies; instead, one learns different things about the writer of each narrative.

One thing that we are not likely to ask, but a white reader of the late nineteenth century may have asked, is how much of his story is true or accurate. For us, this account provides a specific and detailed centerpiece of a large historical picture. We don't doubt its truth because of all the corroborating evidence that has come to light since that time.

For us the larger truth of slavery, of the dignity and accomplishment of Frederick Douglass, is incontrovertible, so we are not likely to question the specifics of his narrative. Nor do they matter. And this is a central question in reading and thinking about people's life stories. When does the truth matter, and which kinds of truth matter?

In the case of Douglass it doesn't really matter, for example, whether it was specifically his aunt or someone else who was brutally beaten. We still learn what we need to learn about the life of a slave.

What comes across is a cohesive story in which the events explain a life and a person. But more important for Douglass's purpose, the life convinces you to believe that slavery should be abolished, and makes real for the reader the experience of being a black slave in the American South. These illuminations are what make this kind of autobiography worth reading.

What, might we speculate, is the process of remembering in which Douglass engaged?

Some vitally interesting questions are raised by his account. First of all, it flies in the face of at least some of the research and claims currently being made about what happens to those who suffer ongoing abuse or other kinds of traumas. It is clear that Douglass not only did not repress or forget sustained abuse, but that it formed the bedrock of his identity and the focal point of his autobiography. Clearly, he did not suffer as much abuse as some of his friends and neighbors did. But, unlike many of the women of Cambodia, for instance, who repressed what they had witnessed during the Khmer Rouge regime and instead developed hysterical blindness from it, Douglass recalled what he had witnessed and could describe it in clear detail:

I have often been awakened at the dawn of day by the most heart-rending shrieks of an own aunt of mine, whom he used to tie up to a joist, and whip upon her naked back till she was literally covered with blood. No words, no tears, no prayers, from his gory victim, seemed to move his iron heart from its bloody purpose. The louder she screamed, the harder he whipped; and where the blood ran fastest, there he whipped longest. He would whip her to make her scream, and whip her to make her hush; and not until overcome by fatigue, would he cease to swing the blood-clotted cowskin. I remember the first time I ever witnessed this horrible exhibition. I was quite a child, but I well remember it. I never shall forget it whilst I remember any thing. It was the first of a long series of such outrages, of which I was doomed to be a witness and a participant. It struck me with awful force. It was the bloodstained gate, the entrance to the hell of slavery, through which I was about to pass. It was the most terrible spectacle. I wish I could commit to paper the feelings with which I beheld it.

Can recent research on how the brain and the limbic system deal with traumatic experiences tell us anything about Frederick Douglass's memory? Researchers such as John Krystal have examined the ways in which people store painful or traumatic memories. They have found, for instance, that the old model of stimulus response has some bearing on the issue. People, like rats, tend to respond adversely to signals or cues that they associate with the original traumatic event. Thus a smell, look, or word can trigger the feelings that were originally created by a traumatic experience. Patients can "vividly re-experience aspects of the traumatic response, while feeling detached from their surrounding environment." Flashbacks may also cause the patient to feel intense emotional responses and panic-like states. Krystal goes on to show that traumatization can alter patterns of memory encoding, leading to the formation of memories with reduced contextual information. Krystal, like many others, claims that traumatic events are often encoded differently by the brain than nontraumatic events. Patients who suffer from what is known as posttraumatic stress syndrome are unusually attuned to cues that might trigger their traumatic memories. These memories, whether recalled or repressed, are known to exert a powerful effect on people's moods, actions, and general health.

And yet, fascinatingly, none of this seems all that relevant to what we know or read of Frederick Douglass's memory. His life seems traumatic and yet cohesive. Moreover, it is possible that by putting his memory to use, it didn't have the paralyzing effect on him it might otherwise have.

Douglass's work shows that several layers of the memory process can be illuminated by the same material. Some aspects of Douglass's situation do a good job of illustrating recent findings in the neural underpinnings of memory. His experiences were considered valuable and important by his peers (other black slaves). Research has shown that events are more likely to be recalled when they are considered socially significant by other members of one's community. For instance, events such as the assassination of President Kennedy are imprinted in people's minds more clearly than other personally relevant or vividly experienced events, because of the public significance. Douglass rehearses the experiences repeatedly first in oral, then in written form. We have known for decades that those events we repeat again and again are much more likely to become permanent parts of our memory store. Douglass's experiences as an adult affirmed the reality and meaning of his childhood recollections. In almost every case, the details of specific events from long ago were corroborated by or consonant with more general knowledge he had about the conditions under which he grew up (slaves were beaten, children were separated from their families, etc.).

We know that one of the ways people check or change their memories is by comparing those incidents to what they know to be logical, possible, and confirmed by evidence. It is hard to maintain certainty about a memory that conflicts everyday logic or is contradicted by a wealth of evidence. We can't know all that went into Douglass's storage, rehearsal, distortion, and cohesive reconstruction of his past. But his three autobiographies suggest that the goal he had in remembering and in putting down his life on paper for others guided not only what he remembered but also what he emphasized, how those events were ordered, and where he directed his audience's attention. Clearly, his life as remembered in his works had a powerful oratorical purpose that may well indeed have ended up shaping the internal life story he represented to himself. Finding three versions of a person's life story in print is a palpable reminder of what we all pay lip service to: there is no such thing as one life story, and each time our life finds expression in a particular narrative it fulfills a purpose that informs both its content and its structure. But his is not the only way to go about remembering a life.

## Disguise — The written life of Philip Roth

There are many reasons to complicate the truth about one's past. Unlike Douglass, who varied what he said about his life in order to make different points to different readers, all in an effort to convince his countrymen to abolish slavery and change their conceptions about black people, Philip Roth wrote about his life in order to confuse his readers and make it clear that knowing a few facts about him didn't tell much at all. As anyone who has read Roth's early novels knows, they practically scream autobiography.

*Portnoy's Complaint,* for instance, depicts the adolescence of a young Jewish boy growing up in New York with a suffocating mother. It describes in hilarious and fluorescent tones his obsession with sex and the frustrations of being a young Jewish man. *Portnoy's Complaint,* and the books that followed it aroused intense feelings, particularly among Jewish readers who felt that Roth was making fun of Jews and American Jewish life. Some also felt that his books revealed everything about him, the writer.

In 1988 he wrote *The Facts,* which he describes as "a novelist's autobiography." It is an answer to his readers about the relationship between his life and his fiction. There are two ways in which he makes the relationship between his life experiences and his fiction the topic of his autobiography. First, he includes a brilliant and complicated conversation between one of his central fictional alter egos, Zuckerman, and Philip Roth—at least as he chose to appear in this book. Second, the chapters of the book are organized around his development as a writer and focus most specifically on experiences that surrounded or explained his work. For instance, the chapter on going to college is really a rumination on his dawning awareness of the ways in which he did and did not identify with his Jewishness. The chapter titled "All in the Family" is a description of Jewish attacks on his work, and one particular episode when he gave a talk, along with Ralph Ellison, at Yeshiva University in New York City. Roth was virulently attacked by members of the audience for being a self-hating Jew. His description is marvelous, particularly his account of becoming increasingly sleepy and vague while on stage in response to the vitriol being directed at him. This event ended up, despite his intentions, becoming the cornerstone of his imaginative resources:

> In midtown Manhattan later, Josie [his wife], Joe [his editor] and I went
> to have something to eat at the Stage Delicatessen, down the street

from the hotel where we were staying. I was angry at what I had
stupidly let myself in for, I was wretchedly ashamed of my performance,
and I was infuriated still by the accusations from the floor. Over my
pastrami sandwich no less, I said, "I'll never write about Jews again."
Equally ridiculously I thought that I meant it, or at least that I should. I
couldn't see then, fresh from the event, that the most bruising public
exchange of my life constituted not the end of my imagination's
involvement with the Jews, let alone an excommunication, but the real
beginning of my thralldom.

Like Douglass, it is hindsight, the ability to retrieve events from the
flow of experience and frame their significance in relations to what
came before and after, that transforms Roth's personal remembering
into autobiography.

Though his book reads in a very direct and open manner, and one
feels that he is speaking to the reader in straightforward, plain ways
about what he has done, thought, and felt, the final chapter, in which
Zuckerman, the character from his previous books, rages at him,
makes it clear that the reader has no way of knowing what is true and
what is not true about Roth the author. He has a disingenuous way of
letting the reader know that everything is slippery. Zuckerman says to
him, for instance, about his earlier description of May, the woman he
lived with after leaving his first wife, Josie,

I don't like the way you treat May either. I don't mean the way you treat
her in life; I don't care about that. I mean the way she's treated as a
subject here. Here you lose your head completely — the poor plebeian
Jew from Newark is so impressed: how calm she was, how patrician she
looked. . . . I don't believe it. Maybe at fifty-five you are suddenly in
love now with those years of your life. But her idealization did not occur
at the time, did it? Her idealization is a necessity of this autobiography.

Roth is telling us not to trust the things we have just read. We are
supposed to put more faith in what his character says to him in front
of us than what he says directly to us. In this way, from a completely
different situation and for different purposes, he — like Douglass —
makes it evident that there is more than one autobiography for any
one life.

Roth's autobiography is written as a companion piece to his fiction. He doesn't indicate an assumption that his life on its own will be

an interesting read. Instead, his autobiography addresses those people who have read his novels. The chapters are not only organized around the writing of novels, they refer to the fiction. The sequence of the chapters, as well as the huge omissions of the book, all point to his emphasis on his life as a writer of the novels he has written. As Elias Canetti has suggested, the only reason to read about an author's life is to illuminate his writing. By the time you have read the apparently clear and direct chapters about his life, and the somewhat more wild and cryptic yet revealing chapter in which Zuckerman rails against Roth, you realize that you knew as much about Roth through his fiction as you do through his autobiography, and that you don't know, nor does he, where events stop and imagination begins.

One of the most interesting findings in recent research on people's life stories is that the telling of your life story can itself influence your life. In her collection of studies, Ruthellen Josselson reports on women who achieve insights through the process of telling an interviewer about their lives, which motivates them to make substantive changes in their lives. For some, this comes about because telling their life stories makes them articulate things that they have never before articulated. For others, putting events together in a sequence causes them to see underlying themes and problems. In some cases the same sequence may also reveal a solution to the problem.

Roth shows us how his fiction, his life, and the writing about his life influence one another. In the end he suggests what many other writers demonstrate: that the best use of their lives is in their writing, rather than in telling directly about it.

## Jamaica Kincaid: Writing a life to transcend it

All of Kincaid's books, like Roth's, have an autobiographical feel to them. And, as with Roth, there are no clear guidelines or clues offered for what is taken from her life and what is simply inspired by her life. What she does say in her recent book, *My Brother,* is that writing about her life saved her from her life. We all know the feeling, and research has supported the reality of this, that telling a story about something that has happened to you can give you relief from the unpleasant feelings you had because of, or during, the remembered event. Jerome Bruner calls this the cooling function of narrative. As noted earlier, James Pennebaker has demonstrated that even for nonprofessional writers, writing down a painful experience decreases people's likelihood of suffering physical maladies in response to the unpleasant event. Putting a bad experience into a story form allows you to distance yourself from it. In addition, you have a chance to rework it, go over it and over it until you understand it, until you can find another way of looking at it, or until it feels comfortable to you. Even the youngest storytellers use stories to solve mental and emotional puzzles embedded within their experiences.

But a writer can take this to a whole other level. Jamaica Kincaid can make something beautiful out of something awful. For instance, in her devastating descriptions of her mother, which run throughout almost all of her books, she takes what was clearly a terribly hurtful relationship and makes something powerful and meaningful out of it. She doesn't transform something sad into something happy. Unlike Zuckerman's accusation that Roth idolized May in his writing of her, Kincaid chooses to describe her mother in almost brutal terms:

> My own powerful memories of her revolve around her bathing and feeding me. When I was a very small child and my nose would become clogged up with mucus, the result of a cold, she would place her mouth over my nose and draw the mucus into her own mouth and then spit it out; when I was a very small child and did not like to eat food, complaining that chewing was tiring, she would chew my food in her own mouth and, after it was properly softened, place it in mine. Her love for her children when they are children is spectacular, unequaled I am sure in the history of a mother's love. It is when her children are trying to be grown-up people — adults — that her mechanism for loving them falls apart; it is when they are living in a cold apartment in New York, hungry and penniless, because they have decided to be a writer, writing to her, seeking sympathy, a word of encouragement, love, that her mechanism for loving falls apart. Her reply to one of her children who found herself in such a predicament was "It serves you right, you are always trying to do things you know you can't do." Those were her words exactly.

The clarity and acuity of her description render it illuminating. In its apparent honesty it takes on aesthetic texture. This is one of the primary functions of autobiography for the writer and the reader. To take experiences whose meaning are too deeply embedded to be understood, give them shape and cohesion in such a way that the meaning becomes manifest. For a writer like Kincaid, putting her life into words has helped her escape the deadening, hurtful, or deforming powers of those experiences:

> I became a writer out of desperation, so when I first heard my brother was dying I was familiar with the act of saving myself: I would write about him.

Like Roth, Kincaid plays constantly with the intermingling of her real and imagined experiences. One of her books is titled, quixotically, *Autobiography of My Mother.* It is clear from her other novels, as well as from straightforwardly autobiographical works such as *My Brother,* that this book represents her attempt to imagine her mother's life. She adds a complex twist by imagining her mother's life had she borne no children. And yet, in many ways it is drawn from what she does know of her mother's existence. Even its title plays with the notion of what autobiography is, and what it does for those who construct it and those who consume it.

This raises the question of what we, the readers, expect from books that seem autobiographical. Just as a jury, a therapist, a friend, or a parent brings specific expectations to a remembering situation, so too the reader construes the remembering exchange in a very particular way. What both Roth and Kincaid play with in their works is the reader's expectation that they will know what actually happened and what the author made up.

In his research on the ways in which memories are created, connected, stored, and lost in the brain, the neuroscientist Larry Squire has shown that one can have a very clear memory without a clear understanding of where the memory comes from. This is referred to as source amnesia. You don't know where you learned or experienced something, though you have a vivid and possibly very accurate mental representation of the content of the memory (what you learned or experienced, for instance). One implication of this is that a person could have a daydream and then store that daydream. Soon it would be a memory rather than a daydream and it might be impossible for the daydreamer to know that the source of the imagined event was a daydream, not a memory. In addition, it turns out that imagining an event and remembering an event involve some of the same neurological mechanisms. So, in effect, researchers have demonstrated what writers have been claiming for a long time—the line between what they make up and what they report is not all that clear. Nonetheless, there is a difference between a book that purports to tell the truth about the past and one that does not. It's just that this difference is more complex than a line between truth and fiction.

## Whose life is it? The reader's role in autobiography

In a piece for the *New York Review of Books,* called "The Awful Truth," Sue Halpern writes about how important readers' expectations are while reading something that smacks of autobiography. She describes the difference between reading Linda Yablonsky's account of her heroin addiction when it was included in a grant submission and was presented as personal history and when she encountered that same material, now presented as a novel *(The Story of Junk: A Novel).* She points out that the dreary mundane details of the writer's addiction were much more engaging and bearable when she thought she was reading something like a diary, but that in novel form they lacked shape and punch. There is no question, as she points out in the same essay, that disgusting or upsetting details are even more riveting when we think we are reading a true story. Of course we don't mean true in the larger sense of illuminating or enlightening. We mean, did these things *really* happen to someone?

Even children as young as 4 respond to the difference between what they think is a true story and something made up. A most delightful example of this occurred when the poet Robert Creeley was reading his poems aloud to a group of elementary school students in New York City in the 1970s. One of the children asked, "Mr. Creeley, are those poems real poems, or did you make them up yourself?" And just as with 4-year-olds, our preoccupation with the distinction does not always mean we know the difference.

It is rare that readers open a book without any expectation of what they are about to read. They have either read something on the book jacket, have read about the book in a newspaper or magazine, or have heard about it on television or from friends. And there is always the title. Every book announces itself and is announced by whatever rumors one hears before reading it. In this way it is rare for a reader to pick up a book without an expectation that it is true or fiction. Within every text there are reminders about the epistemological status of the book: is it made up, is it factual? As Bruner shows in his analysis of

*Billy Budd,* authors remind you that they are the wizards controlling the puppets. But how closely those puppets are based on real people depends on the author of the book. Not only can supposed autobiographies be made up, or embellished, or distorted, but also books presented as novels can actually be thinly disguised autobiographies.

Several psychologists and literary critics have tried to develop models of how the readers' expectations and representations intersect with those of the writer. What is clear from these models is that what you read in a book must be assimilated with what you expect and know when you begin, and that once the words leave the pen of the writer they take on a separate existence, no longer dependent on the intentions and delivery of their author. This must be true in a very particular way when people are reading about the life of the writer. You experience everyone else's autobiography not only in terms of your own narrative expectations but in terms of your own autobiographical experience as well.

We bring to any account of a life our own understanding of how the autobiographical narrative works. If you have been brought up in a community or family that believes, for instance, that early mothering determines what kind of love relationships you are going to have throughout your life, then you are likely to read everyone else's autobiography with an eye toward what kind of mother they had and what kind of early relationships they had.

A friend says,

> I have an easygoing temperament. Let me tell you a story about myself that will show you I have always been that way. When I was little I would get so mad at my mother I would swear to myself that I would never forgive her, that I would keep up a pissy attitude toward her from then on. But I just couldn't do it. After a few hours or a few days, I just had to be nice to her. Just because I have that kind of temperament.

I, raised on a steady diet of psychoanalytic thinking, say to him, "That story is not about temperament. That story is about mother love. You just felt too much passion and longing for your mother to stay mad at her." "Oh no," he says. "That story is about my temperament." He pauses, then adds, "Though, do you want to hear a funny story? Years later when I was a grown up I would go with my wife and children to visit my mother. The minute I got off the ferry after departing from the island where she lived I would be overcome by an insatiable desire for milk." He thinks he has told one story about his temperament and one story about his feelings about his mother. I hear one story, containing two events that are autobiographically related, that reveal a theme in his life story: his feelings about his mother.

In this case the listener's expectation and interpretive framework (mine) redirected the teller's autobiographical narrative. He put together two stories that may never have been put together before, and now a theme is revealed within the events that would never have been identified if not for the listener's framework. In a book, of course, the writer cannot respond flexibly and differentially to various readers and their expectations. But the readers' expectations nevertheless exert influence on the autobiography that lies in front of them. Let us now consider a more literary and therefore pertinent, though possibly less vivid, example.

In Primo Levi's autobiographical account of his imprisonment in a death camp during World War II, *Survival at Auschwitz,* it is hard not to look for clues in the account that explain his survival when so many others perished. He tells you over and over again that he doesn't think there was anything special about him that led to his survival, that it was pure luck, perhaps the luck of having a background in chemistry, which the Nazis found useful. But it is hard not to read the account as an explanation of how and why he survived. Our wish to believe that survival and death can be explained so that we can do something deliberate to ensure one and avoid the other leads us to look for a cause and effect in an account that self-consciously denounces that framework. What we expect in reading his memoir, what we want, is to know that life makes sense. And though Levi's experience of the Holocaust tells him that life doesn't make sense, the very writing of a life story is a sense-making activity.

What the writer thinks or intends and what the reader hears or interprets don't always match up. Nor need they. A published autobiography becomes the mental property of its readers in just as important a way as it is the property of the original rememberer. When a person reads an autobiography, the impressions, narrative, images, and meanings created combine with other thoughts and associations in the mind of the reader. Whenever the reader thinks back on that text she is thinking of the interpreted one in her mind, which is not the same as the one in the author's mind, or even on the page. This is manifested by the fact that people often merge something they have read with something they recall in their own lives. Both types of information are now integrated into one's set of ongoing thoughts. In this way, the autobiography becomes the reader's material, as well as the writer's.

The filmmaker Ingmar Bergman describes the interplay among text, writer, and reader beautifully in the prologue of his account of his parents' early years, *The Best Intentions:*

> This book has not been in any way adapted to the finished film. It has
> had to remain as it was written; the words stand unchallenged and I
> hope have a life of their own, like a performance of its own in the mind
> of the reader.

Even when the writer announces—cryptically or explicitly—the ambiguity in his or her writing between fact and fiction, the reader's expectations strongly shape his or her reading of the material. Take, for example, Mary Karr's *The Liars' Club.* It is written in the first person and announces itself both around and within the text as fact—a clear-cut autobiography. Moreover, in writing about the writing and publicizing of the book, Karr talks about how other people shared their family stories with her when they read her family story, implying that each person—reader and writer alike—were drawing on direct, first-hand experience. She goes to some length to be open about the fallibility of the writing describing other people's lives. She tells us when her sister would disagree with her account of something and talks about her mother's bravery and support when reading Karr's painful and difficult account of growing up with such a mother. And yet, if one pays attention, it is hardly believable as straight autobiography. Many of the descriptions are so precise as to seem beyond the realm of human memory. For instance, her account of being sexually molested by a neighbor who was babysitting has all the precision of imagination and none of the fuzziness or gaps typical in an event remembered from long ago. If this were the case on only one or two specific occasions, we would believe it. After all, recent research has shown that a traumatic memory can be repressed, or alternatively remembered in hyper-detail. But almost all of Karr's account is precise and fresh in a way that seems more like a wonderful imagination than a memory. Moreover, the book is framed by Karr's account of her father's group of friends, called the Liars' Club, who sit around making up things that haven't really happened to them. Is this book her ticket of admission into the Liars' Club?

Students in a course on autobiography were outraged at my suggestion that perhaps not the entire book was based on Karr's actual memories. They felt that if it turned out that some of it were made up, that would represent deceit on Karr's part toward her readers. In a book like this, readers are led to believe, implicitly as well as explicitly, that they are reading a factual account of what the person remembers. On the other hand, we all know that memory is an inherently distorting process. We don't, if we think about it for a moment, think that anyone can offer us a fully factual account of what happened (note the distinction between telling the truth about what happened and telling the truth about what you remember). And yet there is some subtle, perhaps shifting, but nonetheless significant and palpable difference between a deliberately or consciously fabricated account of the past and one that is to the writer's knowledge as accurate as possible.

Mary Karr's book tells us what she thinks about her past. It may not tell us what happened. Her attention to detail, her ability to present the past as if it were sitting there right in front of her at the moment of writing, is one of the things that makes her account so gripping. Ironically, the very narrative device that makes the book seem so real to readers is evidence of the way in which she worked on what might be termed her raw memories. Whatever moments of the past occur to her directly and viscerally have gone through an intensive reworking in order to get them onto the printed page. And it is that skillful and imaginative reworking that makes those memories so palpable and interesting. In one passage, she describes being sexually abused as a child by a young neighbor who is supposed to be babysitting for her. The startling and evocative detail of it illustrates the way in which the craft of writing takes over where memory couldn't possibly supply such meticulous information:

> *I'm not going to hurt you*, he says. Those words hang there in a cartoon balloon above my head. They are an obvious lie, given the man's voice, which has grown an ache in itself, a pleading. *Just open your mouth a little, baby.* I try that. The fleshy head of the pecker parts my lips, easing forward. I open my jaw a little, but am shy of it. My teeth wind up scraping the pecker, so it pulls back with a jerk.

While it is possible that a traumatic experience not repressed instead gets recalled in exquisite detail, almost all of Mary Karr's recollections have this surprising quality of exactness. In describing a memory that she couldn't capture for a long time, Karr reveals, perhaps unwittingly, the process by which she took pieces of the past and turned them into specific, full, cohesive scenes for a book.

> Because it took so long for me to paste together what happened, I will leave that part of the story missing for a while. It went long unformed for me, and I want to keep it that way here. I don't mean to be coy. When the truth would be unbearable the mind often just blanks it out. But some ghost of any event may stay in your head. Then, like the smudge of a bad word quickly wiped off a school blackboard, this ghost can call undue attention to itself by its very vagueness. You keep studying the dim shape of it, as if the original form will magically emerge. This blank spot in my past, then, spoke most loudly to me by being blank. It was a hole in my life that I both feared and kept coming back to because I couldn't quite fill it in.

Karr here is describing herself as the adult, looking backward and trying to bring vague moments from the past back into focus. What she hints at here, and demonstrates throughout her book, is the need to fill in those holes in her memory using her skill as a writer. Her drive to fill in the blank spots in her memory explains not only how she wrote the book, but why she did as well. The motivation for her autobiography is not unlike the motivation in many contemporary memoirs and autobiographies—a kind of self-justification.

## Kathryn Harrison: Autobiography as self-justification

Why did Mary Karr write about her life and what did she want to communicate and accomplish in her book? She knew she had good material and that she could make good material better through her writing. What comes across in her work is that she likes the self that emerges from the book. To write a beautiful book about the hardships of one's childhood is to show one's own heroism: how bad things lead to good things and how the main character transcended or triumphed over adversity. We all are drawn toward reading about people's suffering. And beautiful writing is itself a testimony to the potential for good to come out of bad.

Past experiences may simply provide good writing material for some writers. For many, however, retelling the past is a chance to justify oneself. Certainly Kathryn Harrison's *The Kiss* falls into this category. Harrison's book, like Karr's, reads with a quality of almost painful, certainly arresting, self-revelation. It is an autobiographical account of the sexual relationship she had with her father when she was a young adult. It is told in what appears at first to be an unflinchingly honest and unflattering way. She makes an effort not to win you over, not to pardon herself. And yet, by outlining the emotional wounds inflicted on her by a highly neurotic and hurtful mother and a father who first abandons and then seduces her, the reader is left with no choice but to see her actions as an inescapable result of her earlier experiences. Like Karr, Harrison is at pains to be honest and self-deprecating in her description not only of the past but also in what she reveals about who she is in the present. The wounded self, driven to write, was never merely a victim but a culpable participant, she seems to be confessing. And yet, as Salinger warns us, confessions are never merely what they appear to be. Many autobiographies appear to justify the present by relating it to the past. Those that contain such bleak self-disclosure seem to be a literary version of the hope that confession itself will bring absolution.

In Chapter 4, I described the way in which the drive to make oneself appear good, consistent, and smart leads us all to rearrange events so that we come out looking (and feeling) okay. The written autobiography is simply a more full-fledged and public version of this same dynamic. Just as self-justification in everyday recollection is almost always unconscious, authors may also be unaware that they are justifying who they are or what they have done in the past. Writing does not in itself make the rememberer more aware of the processes of distortion or the motivations underlying the specific memory.

We assume, and many authors tell us, that writing is a form of catharsis, that the readability or salability of the book is an afterthought. But anybody who spends the time and energy it takes to write a book for strangers to buy and read has some more social motivation. As Kincaid herself writes, "for is that not a desire of people who on writing books allow them to be published and exposed to a public; that people who do not know them, absolute strangers, will buy the book and read it and then like it."

In many cases, one might add to Kincaid's sentence, "and then like *me*." For many authors the motivation to tell about one's life is self-serving. Harrison, for instance, is not only working through a traumatic experience, she is also capitalizing on an experience she knows others will want desperately to read about. Finally, and most pertinent from a psychological perspective, she is justifying her own actions by the way in which she writes about them.

Some autobiographies in which difficult childhoods are overcome create a clear and sympathetic path to a difficult adulthood. Connections between the child who suffered psychological trauma and the writing, recollecting adult are made explicit. The reader's attention is drawn toward the implicit pathway between the painful episodes of youth and the troubled writer trying to trace the routes of her demons. There are, however, quite a few autobiographies that are noticeably lacking the telltale signs of self-justification. They seem to serve another social motivation altogether.

## Invitations to peek

Some autobiographies tell the story of lives that hold intrinsic interest for the voyeur in all of us. In at least some of these works, there is little in the way of self-justification and little boasting as well. The writing adult is not explicit. Instead, the reader's attention is drawn almost totally toward the experiencing child, and most particularly toward whatever unusual and distinctive environment in which that child lives. These books seem to rest instead on the curiosity or exotic characteristics of the life lived. Many of them appear to be an invitation toward greater intimacy, as if there were an implicit request on the part of the writer to invite the reader into a world about which he or she might know nothing.

A recent example of this is *Angela's Ashes*, Frank McCourt's account of growing up in the 1930s in Limerick, Ireland. His family was dismally poor. Four of his siblings died from poverty-related illnesses. His father was an alcoholic who was never there. The book is remarkable for its humility. Though it describes abominable poverty and hardship, the reader is never asked to be impressed by the writer, who survived all this. In fact, the adult writer is almost totally absent from the book. This may be why the book gives such an authentic view of what it felt like to be a child. Descriptions that appear to come so genuinely from the child's point of view are part of what keeps such painful accounts from being sentimental. They lack the sentimentality that children lack. The told experiences also offer little in the way of psychological musing or speculation. The reader learns about the child's experience, not the adult's memory. The details of daily life are so far from the details of the commonly lived modern American middle-class life (the life of those most likely to read it). A book like this, based on autobiographical memory but told as if it were a travelogue of childhood and poverty as much as of Ireland, allows one to become more intimate with a specific place and time, as much as with the particular author, or the child he once was.

While I have made a point here of suggesting that most people seek a theme in their life story and organize their autobiography around such a theme or themes, most of us read autobiographies because we want to know the details of other people's experiences. The more vivid those details the better. At least some of the time, we want details that illuminate or corroborate our own experience. This is certainly what Mary Karr found out when she went on the press tour for her book. But equally compelling are the details of lives far different from our own. It seems that we particularly like to read about sad and terrible things, especially since the very writing of an autobiography gives us the cheering knowledge that the writer survived those awful events. This is part of the painful appeal of Levi's book.

An invitation into the exotic, whether because the memories are about a foreign land, a distant time, or the unusual point of view of the young child, is also an invitation to intimacy. The author is asking the reader to peer into his or her particular point of view, the deeply personal details that give meaning to an event situated in time or place. In her memoir *Lost in Translation* (described in Chapter 4), Eva Hoffman writes of leaving Poland for Canada as a 13-year-old. She describes what it feels like to have left Poland and her native language behind:

> The worst losses come at night. As I lie down in a strange bed in a strange house — my mother is a sort of housekeeper here, to the aging Jewish man who has taken us in in return for her services — I wait for that spontaneous flow of inner language which used to be my nighttime talk with myself, my way of informing the ego where the id had been. Nothing comes. Polish, in a short time, has atrophied, shriveled from sheer uselessness. Its words don't apply to my new experiences; they're not coeval with any of the objects, or faces, or the very air I breathe in the daytime. In English, words have not penetrated to those layers of my psyche from which a private conversation could proceed.

Hoffman gives a deeply personal and internal account of what it felt like to leave behind one language (and the place and experiences it conveyed) and have to break into a new language (with all the customs and rules it represented). The reader is made privy to her wrenching sense of loss and the kind of indelible homesickness one can feel for a language and the life embodied within it. Hoffman's rendering of that experience is an example of autobiography as a form of making a connection. She brings the reader into a realm of experience about which they might not otherwise know.

Truth is almost never the issue in autobiographies. The motivations to write autobiographies include persuasion, disguise, self-justification, transcendence, and an invitation into an unknown world of experience. But whenever an autobiography describes subjective experience and depends on the author's memory, we cannot expect to know when it is accurate and when it is not. While blatant lies will eventually be caught, subtle distortions may not. And in any case, the purpose of reading an autobiography is rarely to find out the facts, and as Salinger said, it would be futile to hope for full disclosure anyway.

Autobiographies are the forms of remembering where the deeply personal and the concretely public meet. The most internal and subjective aspects of a memory are given a form that strangers can consume. What may begin as a deeply personal and private experience of a moment from the past becomes transformed into public information. This documentation of the lived life is one way in which people come to share memories. Shared memories constitute the most public and formal use of memory: history.

# CHAPTER SIX

# LAYING CLAIM TO THE PAST: WHEN MEMORIES BECOME HISTORY

## When the personal and the historical converge

A 13-year-old has a small piece of white paper stuck to his wall with a pushpin. On the paper is a pencil rubbing of an engraved name, Jacob Levin. He made the rubbing from the American Immigrant Wall of Honor when, as a 10-year-old, he visited Ellis Island. He hopes it is the Jacob Levin who was his great grandfather, the one who emigrated from Hungary, the one for whom he is named. That scrap of paper makes Jake feel linked to his past. It gives him the illusion that he has a personal, visceral connection to a history he only knows about through others. He has devoured personal accounts of the Holocaust, which offer him something more captivating than simple factual knowledge about what happened to many of his ancestors. They provide him with the details and texture of experience. He doesn't want merely to know what happened. He doesn't wish he had lived through that time, but he does want this particular piece of the past to feel more like a memory and less like history. He wants it to be personal. The distance between knowing about something in history and feeling a more personal, intimate sense of what has happened may be short but nonetheless dramatic. Janet Malcolm writes of her friend, the author Louis Begley,

The author is a fifty-seven-year-old New York lawyer who has not previously written fiction. He and I have been friends for years. I have known that he spent the war years in Poland, but until reading this book, I did not know anything about his wartime experiences; he never spoke of them. After reading it, I begin to know what he must have experienced, since a book like this could not have been written except out of firsthand knowledge of the history it chronicles. The Holocaust is permanently lodged in the unconscious memory of our time.

Malcolm knew about Begley's history before she read his written work about the war, *Wartime Lies*. But she didn't know his memories until she read what he wrote. The psychological difference between knowing and remembering is palpable. One can come at this from the opposite direction as well. We all have a tendency to put ourselves at the center of a recalled event. This has added ramifications when the recalled event has historical significance. A colleague is recalling his father's experiences as a white anti-apartheid activist in South Africa. The father remembers a chilling incident in which a black man who worked for him was murdered in a racially motivated attack. My colleague's father was called to the scene, which was rife with political significance. Several years later, in post-apartheid South Africa, at least 10 different people recall being the one who was called to the black man's side after he was killed. Each person remembers, or wants to be remembered, as the one who was at the center of this incident. Of course, it doesn't change what happened or the significance of those events, which had to do with the horrific treatment of black South Africans under apartheid, and the glaring ugliness of this man's death. But for each person who even might have been there, recalling him or herself at the center makes this piece of history better in some way.

But between knowing about the past and remembering the past lies the complex middle ground—knowing other people's memories. Usually we overlook the nature of how we know what we know about the past. But when it comes to thinking about the past, the source of the knowledge and the type of knowledge one obtains matter a great deal.

Whether talking to a lover or recounting in court, one's memories begin as internal experiences: an image, a fragment of recalled conversation, or a vivid scene. They travel outward and then return to the privacy of one's own mind. The more one has communicated a given memory, the more it becomes a story. The story as told may well take over the initial image, obliterating from one's mind the first visceral moment of remembering. That told story, turned inward, carries with it the reactions of the lover or the juror. It holds the imprint of its life in the outer world. The Soviet psychologist Lev Vygotsky wrote brilliantly about the route language travels, suggesting that words begin in the social realm and then travel inward where they take on private associations and meanings in addition to their culturally shared meanings. But when one's memory is of a historically significant event or era, its fate is quite different. The process of internalizing, assimilating, and using memories that may not be based on direct experience requires its own analysis.

People talk a great deal these days about collective memories and shared history. It is not always clear exactly what they mean. I have spoken at length about the ways in which memories are shaped by the people you share them with, and the situations in which you share them. But ultimately, the memory is a mental representation that resides within a person's mind. What, then, is shared in a shared memory? When people tell us what they recall about a notable event in history—say, a war—we absorb and use their memories differently than we would if they were recalling something that had no shared or larger significance.

Researchers such as Roger Brown, James Kulik, and Ulric Neisser have shown us that people recall historically and socially significant events in a special way. For instance, we know that people seem to recall the assassination of a president in a different way than they would other distinctive moments in their past. Some have described these moments as flashbulb memories, suggesting that a certain moment is imprinted in one's mind and marked as important because of its external significance. Others have suggested that the brain signals its memory mechanism to "print now"; in other words, that at the moment of hearing about something that has potential significance in the larger world, we mark the experience in a special way.

Some studies done on people's recollections of significant events (the *Challenger* tragedy and the assassination of Martin Luther King, Jr., to name two) show that it is only in retrospect as we begin to appreciate the meaning of the event that we rehearse it, and that as we rehearse it we imbue it with the meaning it might have for our cultural community. Ellis Cose, in his book *Color Blind*, writes ironically about the odd assortment of people (among them Newt Gingrich), who invoke the name of Martin Luther King, Jr., in the service of their goals. Cose says, "That King is now a hero to those on both sides of the anti–affirmative-action aisle is arguably a sign of progress. It is also a simple reflection of the fact that the ways in which we remember people often have more to do with our needs than with the actual focus of their existence." When people are recalling a person or event that has significance beyond the person, the intersection between one's own perspective and that of others takes on a different aspect than when one is simply recalling a private and personal event.

There are several ways in which memories bear the impact of others. Chapters 2, 4, and 5 each give examples of the ways in which an audience influences what we recall. Some memories are about events that others recalled as well. For instance, Tobias Wolff and Geoffrey Wolff both recall the same parents and to some extent the same outline of childhood events. In such cases, what is shared are the initial events, not the memory of those events, which may be quite disparate. Finally, there are instances in which one's own representation of an event is deeply influenced by another person's representation of that event, even to the point where one person's memory overlaps with the memories of another person. In intimate settings, these overlapping memories may, over time, become so well told among families or close-knit friends that it seems as if two people literally share the memory, or have identical representations within their memory storage. In his short story "A Curb in the Sky," James Thurber describes, chillingly well, a doting wife who finishes her husband's sentences for him, supplying details to his stories of the past. She even corrects his descriptions of his dreams. Thurber's story is an acid comment on marriage as much as anything else, but it also toys with the line between one person's thoughts and another's, and in that sense brings into relief the important boundary between people's mental worlds.

While married couples and siblings, for instance, may well begin to feel that they remember each other's memories, there is another level at which people's personal constructions of events overlap with a larger, less personal version of that event. In those instances one's vivid personal image, scene, or story illuminates and is illuminated by the larger, more impersonal story of which it is a part. Such is the case, no doubt, for people who have participated in a public and significant event. One's own deeply personal view of the event intermingles with the more general version of that event. In fact, the power of reminiscing together has to do with discovering the points of overlap. In these instances each person has a direct line to the past in question.

What of historical eras or events that are important to many but not experienced by many? As Malcolm points out, the Holocaust has a vivid place in the consciousness of many. But fewer and fewer of us have any personal memory of being in the United States or in Europe during the 1930s. And yet our sense of the Holocaust goes way beyond a date or fact about the past. In what ways do we remember things we never directly experienced?

How should we describe the psychological path that runs between one person's intensely felt memory of an event and a group of people's more generalized version of an event—one they feel familiar with but never actually experienced? Most of us think we know about all kinds of events in history—the signing of the Magna Carta, the Middle Passage, the Declaration of Independence, the civil rights movement, to name just a few. We know that these events happened, we even know details about what happened. But even in the case of relatively recent events, we rarely have personal, direct memories of those events. Instead, we construct an image, scene, or constellation of information that may, if vivid enough, serve as a kind of vicarious memory. We draw on a variety of sources in creating this kind of memory.

Much of the time what we do is to reconstruct an event on the basis of an artifact. Take any monument. For instance, near where I live, in rural southwestern Massachusetts, stands a small stone sculpture of a soldier, adorned with a plaque reading "Shay's Rebellion." It memorializes an uprising of rural farmers in this New England community against the British during the eighteenth century. When I look at that stone figure, it serves as a cue, invoking all the scattered bits of information I have about that time period in rural America, about farm life, and about the American Revolutionary War. I will insert myself in a scene, or imagine it as a movie I am watching. Either way, the statue serves as a cue to a rich array of imagined scenes built around information gleaned from books, movies, and conversation. For another person, the statue remains just that: a static representation of a distant event. What that person sees is dull and lifeless, a statue that simply marks an event which remains an entry in a mental collection of facts.

The potential an artifact has for creating the illusion of memory depends as much on the mental activity of the rememberer as it does on the quality of the artifact. And the artifact is often only a cue, which can only trigger a fuller image if the person has imagination, information, and an eagerness to revisit past events.

Another way we learn about distant and historically significant events is by internalizing the memories of others. Autobiographical memories always have an "I" and, subsequently, an "eye" at the center of them. In fact, Daniel Schacter has shown that there are two positions the eye can take in a memory: central and from the sidelines. You either remember an event as a participant, from within the middle of it, or you remember it from the perspective of an observer, on the edge of the scene. Either way, when several people articulate memories about the same event, a listener who has no direct memory of his or her own can hear several versions each with its own eye, and its own "I" weaving them together into a more general account. When the event is deemed significant by a whole society, we then call this medley of accounts history.

The following excerpt, the recollection of a Japanese man who fought in the war between China and Japan in the 1930s, illustrates one way in which autobiographical memories illuminate and sometimes even form the basis of historical knowledge:

Omiya, Japan — Nearly six decades have passed, but when Shinzaburo Hori sees a baby he still cringes inside, and his mind replays the indelible scene of himself as a young soldier in China, thrusting his bayonet through the chest of a Chinese infant.

Mr. Horie says the killing was unintentional, but the memories follow him everywhere, and he has never mustered the courage to tell even his wife. Nor has he ever told her how as a young soldier, equally inadvertently, he ate the flesh of a 16-year-old Chinese boy.

"I can't forget the fact that I ate a human being," said Mr. Horie, a lean, 79-year-old farmer whose hands trembled as he excavated his war memories. "It was only one time, and not so much meat, but after 60 years I can't put it behind me."

Old men like Mr. Horie all across Japan are still besieged by memories of what they did, and no treaty can end the conflict in their minds and dreams. World War II has also been impossible to lay to rest because disputes about it remain a major cause of friction in East Asia.

What makes Mr. Horie's memory so searing and explosive is the way in which its personal horror converges on an episode that was catastrophic and significant to so many people. To read it is to enter into a scene one would otherwise only know about from outside of the event, as a kind of temporally removed onlooker. Suddenly the reader sees, from inside the scene, what one has only known about in outline, from a distant perspective.

As research has shown, it is quite rare for someone to recall so vividly details that are potentially devastating to the rememberer's self-concept. Mr. Horie seems to have neither repressed nor distorted his memory, even though the memory is damaging to his sense of well-being. Instead, he has kept the memory a secret. This distinguishes him from the masses of people described by most research on the topic, which suggests that people repress unbearable truths about their past, or distort in ways that make those actions seem justifiable. Horie clearly remembers what he did, and hasn't done much to justify it.

Willem Waagenar conducted a study that helps explain Horie's ability to recall these horrendous acts. In the tradition of diary studies so useful to autobiographical memory, Waagenar was his own subject. He kept a diary of daily events, marking not only the time and place but some commentary on the emotional value (from highly positive to highly negative) of various experiences and actions. Subsequently, he returned to this chronicle, using certain cues to see if he could recall the events described in the journal. What he found surprised him and contradicted some work on the self-validation nature of most people's personal recollections: he did, in fact, recall events that were not only negative but disconfirming of his positive self-concept. Waagenar explains that we do, in fact, recall exceptions to our positive self-concepts, and that their saliency, the ease with which we recall them, can at least some of the time be explained by their seeming departure from our usual behavior. If I think of myself as a gentle person and in general remember experiences that confirm this positive self-concept, I am likely also to recall my aberrant behavior on the day that I yelled furiously at my students. Waagenar also proposes that negative actions often have repercussions that are hard to forget and serve as unpleasant but useful reminders of our bad behavior. Clearly, this kind of research can only partly explain something as catastrophic as Mr. Horie's recollections.

The writer of the article about Mr. Horie doesn't tell us the specific circumstances under which Mr. Horie finally revealed these events. If we take Mr. Horie at his word, he has maintained awful memories without ever talking about them. We might assume from what we know about long-term memory that though he never spoke of these horrible events, he did go over them in his mind. It is altogether likely that in some ways the memories were vulnerable to the same mechanisms of forgetting, distorting, and reorienting that extreme or shameful memories undergo. He doesn't reveal much of what he felt in the immediate aftermath of these events, nor does he talk much about how he did or did not integrate these events into his life and his life story. It seems as though he simultaneously maintained the memory and cordoned it off from the other aspects of his self-concept and the ongoing narrative of his life. When he does finally put the memory into words, he relates it to a newspaper correspondent reporting on the war between China and Japan. Thus the context for the memory becomes historical rather than personal. We are not learning about it as part of an interview study of men's retrospective views of what good and bad things have happened in their lives, nor are we learning about it as part of understanding people's guilt-ridden memories. Neither are we learning about it because of some general interest in Mr. Horie's life story. Instead, we are learning about it as part of an inquiry into the legacy of Chinese and Japanese culture.

Why does this focus matter? Because it means that when the reader absorbs Mr. Horie's memory into his or her own mental schema, the context for that information is historical. What does it mean to take in another person's memory and assimilate it into a body of historical facts or images? This in a sense is what we do when we hear about other people's memories of events we only know about because of their historical significance. Mr. Horie remembered what he did because it so violated his ideas and sensibilities and stood out in stark contrast to the rest of his self-image. When we take in Mr. Horie's memory, no sense of self is at the center of our representation of his memory. What reflects on his integrity, morality, and life story reflects for his listeners on the horrors of war. While we may temporarily experience some of his shock and loathing, we don't have to do any mental work to make the story fit with our self-concept. Nor do we have to repress or distort the way we would if it were our own memory. We may weave his memory into our internal narrative of the war between China and Japan. Or we may weave it into a more general representation we have for "the lengths people go to in war," or some such symbolic umbrella. And there may well be personal factors that shape our use of the memory. If a reader has committed similar crimes during a war, he will experience Horie's memory in one particular way. He may feel vindicated or relieved. He may feel sympathetic. Or he may be furious that Horie kept it secret whereas he confessed right away. He may imagine that Horie, like him, uses drugs or liquor to dissociate from the memory. If people of Chinese descent read it, they may feel rage that Horie is allowed to live his life in peace after what he did. For people who have never lived through a war, and have no memories with which to integrate Horie's memory, the process of borrowing is a bit different. They read of Horie's actions with horror, but it's a distant horror. I didn't do the awful things he describes, nor were they done to me. They have no personal reservoir of experience of the time, the terrain, the terror, or the deprivation. The mental context into which they weave Horie's memory are the stories they know of other horrible events and deeds. It is a context of things they know about, not things they have lived through. It doesn't connect to their own memories, only the memories they have borrowed from other people.

Though not a professional historian, I'd like to talk about a few historical events. Knowing about an event and remembering that event are two different things. Somewhere in between these two types of mental experience is the knowledge you can have of an event that you don't recall but others have recalled for you. As a way of unraveling what it means for memories to become part of history, a brief discussion of two events in history—the Holocaust and the Vietnam War—will illustrate a few related points: that memories must find an audience to become part of history, and that historical events often only take shape when several people offer different memories of it. I'll then discuss an event much in the news in 1998 to show how this kind of shared memory/history might develop in the first place.

## Finding an audience for the past

In a kibbutz about 40 miles south of Tel Aviv, there is a small museum dedicated to the memory of the Holocaust. Tom Segev, in his book *The Seventh Million,* writes: "In this place try to see what can no longer be seen, to hear what can no longer be heard, to understand what can never be understood." Knowing what others remember has become an increasingly central part of what we view as historical understanding and the function of memorials. But for the person who lives with terrible memories the private and internal ramifications of remembering are one thing, and the social or political uses of those memories are another.

For those who lived through the Holocaust, and particularly those who survived concentration and death camps, overpowering feelings of secrecy and shame kept them from talking about what they had been through. Many survivors interviewed by Tom Segev talked poignantly about the feeling that they couldn't speak about what they had lived through. One kibbutz member said that he could not speak of the Holocaust to those who had not experienced it:

> After the war, while still a prisoner in a maapilim [illegals] camp in Cyprus, he spent much time thinking about how he would tell people what had happened to him "there," what words he would choose to relate that the Jews of his town were no longer. He felt as if he were the last Jew on earth. When he arrived in the country [Israel] no one asked him, and that was horrible, he said. People did not want to know. The whole period was traumatic, he said.

Segev describes whole communities of survivors who couldn't even talk to one another about what they had all experienced. Living on a kibbutz provided many with a setting in which they could talk about what had happened to them. As many books have documented, and as any visitor to Israel can attest, one might say that the national identity of Israel is built on the notion of memorial. Museums, statues, holidays, and national customs all serve as physical embodiments of Israel's commitment to keep memories of the Holocaust alive and vivid for all who live there. What was so hard for people to talk about in the immediate aftermath of World War II became over time the bedrock of a whole national consciousness.

What does it take for someone to articulate a memory that has seemed too terrible to put into words? The unspoken memory is a different organism from the shared one. For survivors of the Holocaust, their excruciatingly vivid memories were personal. The historical significance, the use of those memories to shape an identity, was something that happened only later:

> For many students and teachers, the Holocaust was a personal trauma. The memories were too harsh, too close, and some of the questions were too distressing to discuss. People who were then in school [right after the war] recall their first encounter with the Holocaust as a kind of

voyeurism — it was a forbidden secret, as discomfiting and tantalizing as death and sex.

The psychoanalyst might ask why people repress when the alternative frees them of symptoms. Many who survived the Holocaust suppressed rather than repressed their memories. The decision (conscious or unconscious) to reveal the past had as much to do with where they lived as it does with any internal psychic balance between the costs of repression and the risk of consciousness. Revealing one's knowledge of a terrible event may have a huge impact on the individual doing the remembering. But much of the time the shift from secrecy to revelation has a great deal to do with what one's neighbors want to or can tolerate hearing.

When it was discovered in 1997 that Madeleine Albright, newly appointed U.S. secretary of state, was of Jewish descent, and that much of her family had perished in Europe during World War II, people wanted to know how this could have been a secret from us, and possibly from her. In explaining why her parents hid their Jewish heritage, Albright's mother explained, "To be Jewish was to risk persecution." She could not have meant this in any concrete way. At the time they were living in the United States, where there was little threat that Jews would be persecuted in any systematic way. But, based on their experiences and those of their family in Europe, their identity as Jews was dangerous to life itself. Albright's mother was explaining in a concrete way what has always been true about those aspects of the past that converge on some larger historical problem or condition. Remembering may in these instances have meaning beyond the personal and psychological.

In his study of Holocaust survivors and their uses of memory, psychologist Henry Greenspan discovered that for many, finding a space or context in which to tell their memories was essential:

> Constrained by both inner and outer silence, their goals become more modest. Survivors like Paula and Leon find more private, limited contexts of recounting. They retell what stories they can, choose the most promising situations for their recounting being heard, and bide their time.

One subject Greenspan interviewed put it this way:

> We didn't talk about it because we didn't want to be different . . . we didn't want to be pointed to as the abnormal people. We tried to get along, you know, "I'm an American too."

To bring out a dark memory and reveal it in the light of day poses internal as well as external risks. Whereas a private memory of childhood may emerge under the gaze of a loving friend or the guidance of a therapist, memories that have historical meaning for the listener emerge in a different kind of context. For each person who has revealed what happened to them during the Holocaust there have been two layers of audience, two spheres of meaning: the personal and immediate, and the social and conceptual.

In his book *Maus*, Art Spiegelman documents his father's story to him of living through the Nazi takeover, imprisonment, and its aftermath. His story is told twice, once to his son and then again to us, his son's readers. And it falls on two kinds of ears, the ears of a son who is finding out what his father endured and why his father is the way he is, and on the ears of his son and the rest of us, hearing the grim details that augment and bleakly enliven what we know about a distant time and place.

Just as Greenspan's subjects say, who you are talking to and what they make of your memories has an important effect on what you will or won't say. Once spoken, those most intimate details of one's past become, in these instances, part of everyone's past. They are no longer memories in the strictly psychological sense because they were never experienced by most of us. And yet, because they are part of our past, because they form the historical context in which we each developed our own more immediate identity, they provide us with a kind of borrowed memory.

The U.S. Holocaust Memorial Museum in Washington, D.C., has embodied this notion. When you arrive at the museum as a visitor, as soon as you pay your entrance fee, you are given a number and name identifying you as an actual victim of the Holocaust. The notion is that your experience of artifacts, demonstrations, text, and photographs will be that much more real and vivid if you are induced to try to experience it through the eyes of someone who actually lived in it. Of course, many of those whose names and numbers are used did not survive the experience. They didn't live to remember it. You are given the momentary illusion that you are remembering it for them.

Elie Wiesel begins his memoir of the Holocaust by telling us about what someone else heard and saw of the concentration camp. His description of his childhood experience of the Holocaust begins with the story of Moshe the Beadle, an innocuous neighbor liked by all. Then one day during the early part of the war, Moshe was transported along with other Jews from Wiesel's hometown. Wiesel recalls quickly forgetting about the deportees, assuming that they were happily resettled in another region. However, Moshe returned with horrific stories of what he had seen—Nazi soldiers ordering the Jews to dig massive graves and then calmly and methodically killing the deportees and dumping their bodies into the graves. Moshe tells all this to young Wiesel. This is, we are led to understand, his first intimation of what is to come, and it is ours too.

Wiesel begins his memoirs by looking through the eyes of another, just as we begin to learn about a past we didn't experience by looking through Weisel's eyes. In that sense, his opening passages capture what all memory is as it is transformed from personal autobiography to everyone's history.

When we read about other people's experiences, we borrow their memories. Doing so gives us a sense of immediacy, texture, and insight that we could never acquire through objective accounts and artifacts alone. In addition, each memory carries with it other kinds of information, an aura of the past that gives us a broader sense of that time and place. The literary critic Mikhail Bakhtin has talked about this in a somewhat different context. He argues that any speaking character in a book (his most vivid examples are from the fiction of Dostoyevsky) gives voice to the perspectives, cultural habits, and characteristics of many people—in other words, each character is polyphonic. Bakhtin demonstrates the ways in which a character's words and phrases carry with them nuances, meanings, associations, and connotations that may reflect whole sectors of a society.

When we hear about someone's past we hear not only about that person, but also about the time that he or she recalls. In this way all kinds of memories are historical. In a stunning piece on not being able to remember his mother's voice, a writer talks about what we do and don't recall of the personal past, and what is and is not carried along with that thread of memory:

> My mother's mother said "pie-anna" for "piano." Like her daughter, she sat at that instrument between intervals of housework and played hymns. Her voice had the reediness that comes after a hard life. I know a lot of things about my grandmother, but they are things a child knows, not adult information. I don't know a single sentence her parents ever spoke to her. My mom learned in school not to say "pie-anna," and I would wager that she never once used a phrase that

was uniquely hers. She spoke, as we all do, a temporal dialect – a speech made up in the main of plain, enduring words but also of short-lived phrases that belong to a place and a moment.

The writer tells us he cannot recall his mother's voice. But he can recall the way that his mother's mother said certain words. Over time, what is recalled of one's past shifts? For this writer it is the historical context rather than the real people that is most easily evoked. But it reminds us that when we remember the past or visit someone else's memories, it gives us a view of a whole era, a community, a way of living beyond the specific events recalled. This, clearly, is one important way that people's individual memories offer the rest of us history.

The memories and autobiographies about the Holocaust discussed here all tend to converge on a common view of what happened. They don't, any longer, change what we know of what it was like for a Jew to live or die in the war, nor do they change what we think about those events. What they do is to give us a feeling of detail and immediacy, and evoke a level of emotion that no mere historical account could. In these instances, borrowing other people's memories brings us into the experience in a unique way and, therefore, changes our access to a historical event. When people talk of shared memory in a situation such as this, they are talking about a version or view of an event that people hold in common. The idea is that each person in the community, group, or society has an overlapping or similar narrative or collection of details and facts about an event. But not all shared memory involves convergence or similarity of representations. The psychologist Daniel Wegner has written lucidly and convincingly about another way in which people can remember collectively.

## Converging perspectives

Wegner suggests that people have been trying to explain collective thinking for a long time. Turn-of-the-century explanations of collective thinking resorted to the notions of inherited thoughts or the supernatural. But the advent of behaviorism pushed all of that out of the way with its focus on the individual learning through specific experiences. How, then, in an era of empirical psychology and a firm idea of the individual, do we explain shared memories? Wegner argues that we have to look at the phenomenon in a new way. Instead of assuming that shared memory must involve a group of people all thinking or remembering the same event in the same way, he shows how groups of people exchange information about the past. What they know together is more than what any one of them knows alone. Part of his argument rests on the simple but striking insight that much of our remembering is embodied in forms outside of the mind: writing, memorials, pictures, and lists. It is the norm, rather than the exception, for us to fill in our internal representations of past events with information gleaned from these outside forms, including what other people can tell us.

In one study Wegner and his colleagues asked intimate couples to remember long lists of information. In each list some of the information drew on the expertise of the woman in the couple, and other information rested on the expertise of the man. Wegner showed that the couple acted as a team, each spontaneously taking responsibility for the terms they would most easily remember. Wegner calls this kind of collaboration transactional memory. One of the interesting implications of his work is that people can have dissimilar memories of an event, or remember the event from different perspectives. The picture of that event that develops across people will be richer and more complex than the view any one of those people might have. The Vietnam War offers an interesting though troubled example of this phenomenon.

The situation in Vietnam, as almost every American over the age of 30 knows, was viewed from wildly divergent, even harshly conflicting points of view. Most people either ardently supported or violently disagreed with our military involvement in Indochina during the 1950s, 1960s, and early 1970s. At the time, our sources of information were skewed, to say the least. We only knew what the United States government would tell us. Few men coming back from the war in the early years would say much about it. Then the antiwar movement picked up momentum and we began to get a different picture of both the rationale (or lack of one) for being there and facts about what was happening there. Now, in retrospect, there have been two divergent sorts of memories the rest of us could draw on in thinking about that piece of our past. Some of the most compelling and disturbing information comes from men who fought in the war but only began communicating their experiences long after. This material has been made into several movies, all very potent in their effect—*Platoon, Apocalypse Now, The Deer Hunter, Born on the Fourth of July*, to name a few. However, each of those movies is so entwined with the imaginations of the filmmakers that it is hard to separate recollections.

There are, however, some notable books that draw from the memories of individuals, giving us entrée into a kind of memory of Vietnam that changes the way we think about the war. Preeminent among those books is the writing of Tim O'Brien. In his collection of connected stories, *The Things They Carried*, O'Brien gives a visceral and compelling account of what it was like to be in the war. It is also, inevitably, a rumination on the nature of memory and truth. Like Holocaust survivors, American soldiers who were in Vietnam felt (and some still feel) that their experiences were shameful in some way. During the war they were surrounded by the silence of terror. And, like survivors of the Holocaust, many Vietnam veterans felt that once they returned home they were wrapped in a second kind of silence: the silence of a group of people who didn't really want to know. And like Holocaust survivors, they needed to tell as a way of surviving. Although the circumstances of their ordeal and the proximate causes of their subsequent sense of shame differed dramatically, they felt pressure to keep silent about horrendous experiences and the concomitant internal drive to tell those experiences to others is comparable.

Memories, and the stories in which they are wrapped, that come from people like Tim O'Brien allow us to smell and feel the stench or terror, the horror and desolation felt by young men totally disoriented by their presence in Vietnam.

> Forty-three years old, and the war occurred half a lifetime ago, and yet the remembering makes it now. And sometimes remembering will lead to a story, which makes it forever. That's what stories are for. Stories are for joining the past to the future. Stories are for those late hours in the night when you can't remember how you got from where you were to where you are. Stories are for eternity, when memory is erased, when there is nothing to remember except the story.

In 1994, an extremely important player in the decisions and actions carried out during the Vietnam War, Robert McNamara, published an autobiography presented as a kind of *mea culpa*. This too is a memory, but of a very different sort. To read McNamara's account and read an account such as Tim O'Brien's is to engage in what Wegner calls transactive memory—only to do so at a literary remove. McNamara's book, *In Retrospect,* begins with a chapter that recounts his early life. This is presented as a kind of foreshortened path that leads you directly to his life in government. The rest of the book describes his involvement with the Kennedy, Johnson, and Nixon administrations as it pertained to his role in the country's military activity in Indochina.

Unlike a book such as O'Brien's, which brings you into an experience through all your senses and emotions, McNamara's is a revelation of discussions and information that no one from within had yet told. It is what we learn, not what we are made to experience, that is important about his memoir. The most important point in his book is his admission that he and his colleagues never really thought through whether they had a chance of achieving their military or political aims through military involvement in Vietnam. Equally stunning is his admission that he came to believe years before the actual U.S. withdrawal that such an action should be taken. At the end of the second edition of the book is an intriguing collection of letters and other responses notable people had to the publication of the book. These reactions allow us to see how people responded to this important addition to our transactive, or collective, body of memories regarding the war. Some who wrote were impressed that McNamara was courageous enough to admit a mistake that had such catastrophic consequences for millions of people here and in Southeast Asia. Others were infuriated that he dared complain of sleepless nights and guilt that couldn't compare, in the writers' view, to what young men and their families went through as a result of the "mistakes" McNamara made all those years ago.

Many, if not all of the people writing, seemed already to know most of what McNamara was admitting in his memoir. And yet, having him recount it as a personal story changed its place in the body of information we consider to be our collective memory of Vietnam. This has in part to do with the power of hearing about the past from someone's specific point of view. Having McNamara say it, and say it in the form of a memoir, gives it a force that it didn't have when presented as pieces of authorless, subjectless information. As the layperson pieces together an account of the Vietnam War, she or he must integrate a retrospective view such as McNamara's with the kind embodied in Tim O'Brien's writing.

Life as we live it in the United States at the end of the millennium presents a special, perhaps paradoxical, context for historical remembering. On the one hand, we live at a time when there is unprecedented interest in the experience of the individual. Memoirs and autobiographies abound. Readers are drawn in by subjective accounts of events, and we place high value on the reports and accounts of eyewitnesses. On the other hand, we are surrounded by events that, while having obvious historical significance, are not directly experienced by anyone. This means that we are constantly looking for ways to grasp personal and direct experiences of ourselves and others. At the same time, we try to do this with events with which we have had only indirect encounters.

Newspapers provide one of the best sources of data for examining the strange intersection of personal and public memory of historical events. Newspaper reports embody one current way in which people encounter events, perspectives, and one another. Each day, one can find examples in a newspaper of events unfolding. The articles describing these events not only tell what has been recalled and recorded of the past, they are themselves artifacts for future generations. They demonstrate what people (the journalists) want to tell about events, and they show equally well what it is readers want to know about events. Moreover, increasingly, the articles constitute one physically real and concrete form of externalized memory, the kind that Daniel Wegner talks about.

Take, for example, a curious event unfolding as this book is being written: Special Prosecutor Kenneth Starr's investigation into allegations that President Bill Clinton conducted a sexual relationship with White House intern Monica Lewinsky and then encouraged her to lie about it under oath. In this case (as with others that bear similarities, such as the confirmation hearings of Supreme Court Justice Clarence Thomas, during which Anita Hill testified that Thomas engaged in sustained and serious sexual harassment), what we will remember is not what happened, because only two people were directly involved in whatever did or didn't happen; instead we will remember the news reports themselves. At the time of this writing, it is not at all clear how the Clinton episode will play out, and what the conclusion—if there is one—will be. That is why I choose it as psychological data to examine. Choosing this example reflects an old and marvelous tradition among psychologists to seize events as they are unfolding, when those events provide us with natural experiments far more interesting, and certainly more relevant, than any we could create in a laboratory. For our purposes, the event and its eventual truths or conclusions are less important than the ways in which the average person takes in information and puts together something that might someday be called historical memory.

## The process of creating historical memories

As I write this chapter, Bill Clinton, the current president of the United States, is under intense scrutiny by the public, the press, and a special prosecutor. Each day new accounts come out in the news about what Clinton has or hasn't done. It is a fascinating study in how perspectives, information, innuendo, and personal biases shape the public memory of an event. First some background.

Several years ago it appeared that Clinton might be guilty of some unethical, possibly illegal, actions in relation to an investment he and his wife had made in a land development named Whitewater. A special prosecutor, Kenneth Starr, was designated to investigate these wrongdoings. Meanwhile, a woman named Paula Jones accused Clinton of sexual harassment while he was serving as governor of Arkansas. Soon Starr began making links between the target of his investigation, Whitewater, and the accusations of Paula Jones. In January of 1998, *Newsweek* reporter William Isikoff learned that a woman named Linda Tripp had tape-recorded telephone conversations between herself and a young friend, Monica Lewinsky. It seemed that Monica had talked to her friend Linda Tripp about an affair she had been having with someone who seemed to be Bill Clinton, while Clinton was president and Lewinsky was an intern in the White House.

Starr proceeded to subpoena Lewinsky to appear before a grand jury to testify about whether she had indeed had a sexual relationship with Clinton, in the White House, and whether in fact he had at any time urged her to lie about the affair if she were to appear before a court of law. For over a week, the nation was in such a paroxysm of judgment, horror, concern, and prurient fascination that not even the news of the Pope's historic visit to Cuba or an impending clash with Iraq over arms inspections could distract Americans from what they wanted to know about Clinton's behavior with Monica Lewinsky. To watch the news and converse about the news as the events unfolded was literally to see a historically significant shared memory in the making.

One of the things most striking about the unfolding of the Lewinsky/Clinton case is that everything most of us will learn about this historical event is going to be from accounts we see on television, hear on the radio, or read in magazines and newspapers. Almost no one will have a personal, visceral experience to remember and describe. Therefore, whatever shared memory there will eventually be of the event will be the memory of media, not the memory of an experience.

One of the most alarming aspects of this news as it unfolded was the difficulty the average reader had in deciphering established facts from unconfirmed rumors. Somehow the distinction between the two was almost completely obliterated in the initial reporting. In fact, 10 days after the story broke, the *New York Times* presented a chart showing which "facts" had come from where, and suggesting that many of the details that people were thinking of as fact were actually without any firm basis. But, by the time this report came out, the *New York Times,* along with most other newspapers and magazines, had so blurred the lines between different types of data that the American public was walking around with a template of the event that put rumor and fact together.

One of the details that made all this so complicated was that central to the possible case against Clinton were the recorded conversations between Lewinsky and Tripp. Many of the reports that subsequently came out about the issue were based loosely on what was reported or supposed to have been on those tapes. But in fact, *Newsweek* reporters, who had gotten the tapes, had only listened to 90 minutes of tape-recorded conversations from a total of $18\frac{1}{2}$ hours that Tripp had recorded. From those 90 minutes, *Newsweek* printed what it considered to be the relevant portions, which when read aloud added up to approximately 6 minutes of conversations. And yet many of us reading about Lewinsky and Tripp in the paper felt that we were reading information gleaned directly from vast amounts of raw data (the taped conversations). This was not the case. And many supposed facts about the case were not only not facts, they weren't even substantiated hearsay. For instance, it was alleged, and reprinted, joked about, and discussed in almost every household in America, that Mr. Clinton and Ms. Lewinsky engaged in oral sex, and only oral sex. Jane Fritsch, in an article in the *New York Times* explains that rumor in the following passage:

> Third-hand news reports at best. The *Los Angeles Times* quoted a source who said he had listened to tapes of conversations between Ms. Lewinsky and Ms. Tripp. The *Times'* article contained no direct quotes from the tapes, but paraphrased the source, who is not identified in any way that might indicate what his biases might be. Ms. Lewinsky is heard saying that she engaged only in oral sex with the President, the article said.
>
> *Newsweek* also paraphrased the tapes on this point, saying that Ms. Lewinsky said Mr. Clinton preferred oral sex. But it offered one direct quote from Ms. Lewinsky: "there was no penetration." The *Newsweek* story implies, but does not state outright, that *Newsweek* has heard the

section of tape that contains this discussion. But *Newsweek* reporters
did not hear that recording, according to Ms. McDaniel (Washington
Bureau Chief for *Newsweek*).

In following the news reports regarding the Clinton/Lewinsky case, one sees an event that did or did not occur between two people transformed into a series of interrelated narratives and communications that make up a story. It is this story that will be recalled and viewed as history, not the interchange itself. The relay and consequent changes of information that have occurred in the representation and communication of the story is a naturally occurring demonstration of Frederic C. Bartlett's early studies on the social transmission of memories. His work showed that as a story is passed along within a cultural community it is changed in ways that reflect the concerns and values of the culture. But this modern exemplification of his idea adds a new facet to Bartlett's original argument. As history is being made about Clinton, the stories people tell and remember about what happened have already been filtered through what was reported. These reports are themselves already filtered in most cases through hearsay, rumors, and other people's reports. In this way, little modern history is based on the passing down of firsthand reports of experiences. In the case of Clinton the following kinds of information might go into such a thing as shared memory:

1. The fact of it: President Clinton has been accused of having an affair with a White House intern.
2. There is suspicion that he urged her to lie under oath about that affair.
3. There was a media blitz about it.

But, as we know, a few facts do not a memory make. Nor do they make history. It is the fleshing out of those facts, the elaboration of a fact into a story, that makes it history.

How much perspective, detail, description, and subjectivity is in that pseudomemory will be determined by a host of factors. One such factor concerns the amount of time that elapses between the individual narratives we each piece together and some more cohesive and objective account that emerges for public perusal. In addition, how strongly we feel about it may well have to do with the ways in which Clinton's or Lewinsky's situation touches on details or dilemmas in our own lives. Also relevant is what our overall view of the president and the presidency is. As Elliot Aronson has claimed, if you are happy with the state of the nation and you attribute that at all to the president, then you are going to be inclined to rationalize his behavior and claim that his private life is none of our business. If you are unhappy with the state of the nation, or hate him for other reasons (philosophically opposed to a Democrat, mad at him for past behaviors, etc.), then you will likely see him as a villain in the current circumstance. This in turn will make you more likely to believe the things you read about him, and suspend analysis of the source of the information you receive.

We record our experiences through words and symbols. Psychologists are still arguing about what that form of mediation is. Words, images, activation, and deactivation of neuronal groups are three non-mutually exclusive possibilities. When you live in a world in which much of what you experience is experienced secondhand, through television, books, newspapers, and oral reports from others, there are two levels of mediations that need to be accounted for: the one in your own head and the one that is used for the memory transaction. Imagine it, as Bartlett did, as a relay system. Each time gets wrapped in layers of representation; each representation occurring at the moment the event is communicated to yet another person. At each relay station something gets added to the event.

As another example of this, consider a recent description of a collection of small engraved cylinders made of stone that were used in Mesopotamia 6,000 years ago, now available for viewing at a museum. These cylinders, when rolled across clay, create an imprint that was then used as a seal for a container. The article describes the way in which one particular scholar, Edith Porada, studied these cylinders and brought them to life:

> The cylinder seals lie inert in their cases. Their images make no sense until rolled onto clay, or rather they make no sense until they have been impressed upon a mind that can bring them to life again . . . she [Porada] is done now, but the seals remain, entwined forever with her words.

In a sense, memory always involves the transferal of images, information, and words from one place to another. In most cases the transferal is a complex process involving many steps. Those seals only become history as they travel from the cylinders to the clay, through the insights and understanding of the historian onto a written page that other historians can read, or in this case that can be communicated to a wide audience through newspaper reportage.

Paradoxically, as more and more of our lives are lived indirectly through these complex layers of representation and media, we became thirstier than ever for accounts of direct experience, experience that remains, or has become to a greater extent, the central focus of our historical curiosity. Let me give you yet another newspaper example. Consider a recent article in the *New York Times,* reporting an account describing the murder of Gandhi in 1948. This account is timely because the Hindu Nationalist Party is having a resurgence in India, and it was members of that party that assassinated Gandhi. What makes the article stand out is that it focuses on the recollection of one of the assassins, the brother of the man who actually fired the shots that killed Gandhi, and he was instrumental in planning the assassination. The article states,

> Gopal Godse offered a razor-sharp recollection of his own role in the killing, from the moment when Nathuram Godse asked him if he would take part — "I gave my consent immediately" — to a first botched attempt on January 20, 1948, 10 days before the assassination.

The article ends with a quote from Godse, one that casts the events from a personal, if shocking, even repellent, perspective:

> Pausing for a sip of sugar tea, Mr. Godse added: "So you see, it is not as if we had gone to New Delhi to steal Gandhi's watch. That would have been a sinful, dirty thing. But that was not the case. We killed with a motive, to serve the highest interests of our people."

This personal view of a public event and a personal construal of the meaning of the event draws us in, gives us perhaps a new way of remembering the event. What we end up with is a representation of a multiplicity of perspectives on the event, each incomplete but tagged with a personality, a viewpoint (the original news accounts, the accounts in biographies and movies of Gandhi, and now this—an account from one of Gandhi's antagonists). In this case we are given a sense not only of what one participant thought and said but also of how he views the event in retrospect. The reader doesn't have to agree with or internalize that point of view to be affected by it. Imagine several people looking together at a film of the past. Each has his or her own perspective on the event. Now imagine that each person can look at the film the other has created in his or her mind. They see the event and the kinds of thoughts and reconstructions that reveal themselves in the process of reminiscing. Thirty years ago in their groundbreaking work on narratives of personal experience, William Labov and Joshua Waletzky argued that every narrative contained a commentary. As we view and internalize other people's memories, now calling it history, we also record the layers of commentary that come with those versions of the past.

This book started with the notion of a vivid moment of recollection traveling outward into the world of people and back again into the mind of the rememberer, and it ends with the notion that people's memories cross all kinds of boundaries. Memories take us from within our own retrospection to the space between two people; from the most private and informal settings such as a bedroom to the most formal and public settings such as a courtroom. Moments of the past can be expressed in ways that are idiosyncratic and transient, such as a conversation, as well as in ways that are permanent and generalized, such as a history book. We constantly revise our own recollections in response to what others think and say and feel. We also borrow recollections as a way of feeling that we know what has happened in the past. In this sense memory is at once the most deeply personal and private aspect of experience and simultaneously the means by which we extend ourselves beyond our own mental boundaries.

# NOTES

CHAPTER 1: WHERE MEMORIES BEGIN

Page 3: Perhaps the most readable and comprehensive overview of both classic and current findings in memory research can be found in Daniel Schacter, *Searching for Memory* (New York: Basic Books, 1996). A good introduction with a biological perspective is Stephen Rose, *The Making of Memory* (New York: Anchor Books, 1992).

Pages 3–4: The story I've described is the title story in Delmore Schwartz, *In Dreams Begin Responsibilities* (Norfolk, CT: New Directions, 1938).

Page 4: A short but excellent description of what we have learned recently about memory can be found in *The Observer,* published by the American Psychological Society. The study discussed here is "The Nature (and Fallibility) of Memory" (February 1998), p. 13. *Current Directions in Psychological Science,* 6(3) (June 1997), also contains timely and well-written accounts of some of the most interesting new research in memory.

Another excellent collection of recent findings about memory can be found in *Memory Distortion,* edited by Daniel Schacter (Cambridge, MA: Harvard University Press, 1995). Gerald Edelman, *The Remembered Present* (New York: Basic Books, 1989), contains his argument that remembering and imagining draw on the same neural pathways, and thus are more similar than we think.

Page 5: One excellent summary of the information processing model of memory can be found in Henry Gleitman, *Psychology* (New York: W. W. Norton, 1986). A classic that describes this model is the chapter by R. C. Atkinson and R. M. Shiffrin, "Human Memory and Its Control Processes."

In *The Psychology of Learning and Motivation,* Vol. 2, edited by Kenneth and Janet Spence (New York: Academic Press, 1968). Another classic is Donald Norman, *Models of Human Memory* (New York: Academic Press, 1970).

Three current books that present differing views on the validity and nature of repressed memories are Lenore Terr, *Unchained Memories* (New York: Basic Books, 1994); Elizabeth Loftus and Kathleen Ketcham, *The Myth of Repressed Memory* (New York: St. Martin's Press, 1994); and Richard Ofshe, *Making Monsters* (New York: Scribner, 1994). A fourth, which offers more of an overview, is Matthew Erdelyi, *The Recovery of Unconscious Memories: Hyperamnesia and Reminiscence* (Chicago: University of Chicago Press, 1996).

Page 6: Schacter's *Searching for Memory* gives an excellent account of the constructive nature of memory. So do two collections edited by Ulric Neisser: *Memory Observed* (New York: W. H. Freeman, 1982), and *The Remembered Self,* edited with Robyn Fivush (Cambridge: Cambridge University Press, 1994).

Page 7: Two excellent collections of papers on children's memory are *Memory Development in Children,* edited by Peter Ornstein (Hillsdale, NJ: Lawrence Erlbaum Associates, 1978)—though old by scientific standards, it does a fine job of laying out the issues, many of which are still unresolved; and *Memory Development in Children,* edited by Robert Kail (New York: W. H. Freeman, 1990). A more current volume is *Knowing and Remembering in Young Children,* edited by Robyn Fivush and Judith Hudson (Cambridge: Cambridge University Press, 1990). An excellent essay is Katherine Nelson, "The Psychological and Social Origins of Autobiographical Memory," American Psychological Society, 1993.

Endel Tulving's work is described in more papers on memory than can be counted. One succinct account of the basic idea can be found in the article, "Recall and Recognition of Semantically Encoded Words," *Journal of Experimental Psychology,* 102 (1974), 778–787. Another good account can be found in Tulving's, *Elements of Episodic Memory* (New York: Oxford University Press, 1983).

Page 9: Ann Brown's most famous paper on meta-memory is probably "The Development of Memory: Knowing, Knowing about Knowing and Knowing How to Know," in *Advances in Child Development and Behavior,* Vol. 10, edited by H. W. Reese (New York: Academic Press, 1975).

An interesting and now classic look at this issue is in M. Cole, J. Gay, J. Glick, and D. Sharp, *The Cultural Context of Learning and Thinking* (New York: Basic Books, 1971). Another excellent account is Michael Cole and Sylvia Scribner, "Cross Cultural Studies of Memory and Cognition," in *Perspectives on the Development of Memory and Cognition,* edited by J. W. Hagen (Hillsdale, NJ: Lawrence Erlbaum Associates, 1977).

Page 10: Richard A. Lewontin's work on the interaction of genes and environment offers a powerful model of what is sometimes now called emergent processes. One good source is his book *Human Diversity* (San

Francisco: Scientific American Books, 1982). The quote is from Claudio Stern of Columbia University, *New York Times,* September 2, 1997, p. C1.

Page 11: The quotation is from Penelope Lively, *Jacaranda, Oleander: A Childhood Perceived* (New York: HarperCollins, 1994).

The piece that describes the words of Mrs. Mudd was written by Ralph Gardner, *New York Times,* January 30, 1992, p. C1.

Page 12: Mary Karr, *The Liars' Club* (New York: Viking Press, 1995).

Page 13: Tom Segev, *The Seventh Million* (New York: Farrar, Straus & Giroux, 1993).

Luis Buñuel, *My Last Sigh* (New York: Knopf, 1983), p. 60.

Page 14: Kathryn Harrison, *The Kiss* (New York: Random House, 1997).

See Donald Spence, *Narrative Truth and Historical Truth* (New York: W. W. Norton, 1982).

Page 15: Neisser's false recollection of the news of Pearl Harbor can be found in "Snapshots or Benchmarks?" in *Memory Observed,* edited by Ulric Neisser (New York: W. H. Freeman, 1982).

The study on source amnesia was reported in *The Observer* (February 1998), Report 6.

Page 16: A whole section in *Memory Observed,* edited by Ulric Neisser (New York: W. H. Freeman, 1982), is devoted to papers on the performance of memory, including the work of A. Lord, W. D'Azavedo, and G. Bateson. Another interesting account can be found in David Rubin, *Memory in Oral Traditions* (Oxford: Oxford University Press, 1995).

Page 18: Shelley Taylor's book, *Positive Illusions* (New York: Basic Books, 1989), describes the ways in which we lie to ourselves about the past to stay healthy. A briefer account can be found in Roy Baumeister, "Lying to Yourself—The Enigma of Self-Deception," in *Lying and Deception in Everyday Life,* edited by M. Lewis and C. Saarni (New York: Guilford Press, 1993).

Page 19: The idea that a painful experience can be eased by putting it in story form is discussed in Jerome Bruner, *Actual Minds, Possible Worlds* (Cambridge, MA: Harvard University Press, 1986).

One good account of Peggy Miller's theory and the work that demonstrates it is, "Narrative Practices in Self-Construction," in *The Remembering Self,* edited by Ulric Neisser and Robyn Fivush (Cambridge: Cambridge University Press, 1994).

Page 21: Peter Gay's second volume in his trilogy on Victorian Europe, *The Naked Heart* (New York: W. W. Norton, 1995), examines the Western focus on the self.

## CHAPTER 2: MEMORIES CREATED IN CONVERSATION

Page 24: *Letters of Rainer Maria Rilke,* edited by Jane Bannard Greene and M. D. Herter (New York: W. W. Norton, 1945), letters from 1906 to 1907.

Page 25: Leo Tolstoy, *Anna Karenina,* translated by Constance Garnett (New York: Bobbs-Merrill, 1978), p. 428.

Page 26: Emily Brontë, *Wuthering Heights* (New York: Buccaneer Books, 1976); Boris Pasternak, *Dr. Zhivago* (New York: Pantheon Books, 1958).

Pages 26–27: A wonderful account of Daniel Stern's theory of mother-child interaction can be found in his book *The First Relationship* (Cambridge, MA: Harvard University Press, 1976). The great classic on this topic is John Bowlby, *Attachment and Loss, Vol. 1, Attachment* (New York: Basic Books, 1969).

Page 27: Another excellent collection of papers on the development of children's memory is *Children's Memory: New Directions in Child Development*, No. 10, edited by Marion Perlmutter (San Francisco: Jossey-Bass, 1980).

Page 28: For a discussion about the absence of elaborated recollection of experiences and events, see R. V. Kail and J. W. Hagen, eds., *Perspectives on the Development of Memory in Children* (Hillsdale, NJ: Lawrence Erlbaum Associates, 1977).

The great early book on scripts is Roger Schank and Robert Abelson, *Scripts, Plans, Goals and Understanding* (Hillsdale, NJ: Lawrence Erlbaum Associates, 1977). Another excellent and more current book is Katherine Nelson, *Language in Cognitive Development* (Cambridge: Cambridge University Press, 1996).

Page 29: For a summary of studies on the social interactions between parents and children, see Susan Engel, *The Stories Children Tell* (New York: W. H. Freeman, 1995).

Page 31: For chidren's ability to reconstruct past events, see R. V. Kail, *The Development of Memory in Children* (New York: W. H. Freeman, 1990). Also see Peter Ornstein, ed. *Memory Development in Children* (Hillsdale, NJ: Lawrence Erlbaum Associates, 1978).

An excellent description of Elizabeth Loftus's seminal study on children's susceptibility to false memories can be found in her article "Memory for a Past That Never Was," *Current Directions in Psychological Science*, **6** ( June 1997). In that same issue is another excellent description, by Maggie Bruck and Stephen Ceci, "The Suggestibility of Young Children."

Pages 32–33: This study, by Jessica Jungsook Han, Michelle D. Leichtman, and Qi Wang of Harvard University, is titled "Autobiographical Memory in Korean, Chinese and American Children." At the time of this writing it was not yet published. Another paper on this topic is M. Mullen and S. Yi, "The Cultural Context of Talk about the Past: Implications for the Development of Autobiographical Memory," *Cognitive Development*, **10** (1995), 407–419.

Page 33: Hazel Markus and Shinobu Kitayama, "Cultural Variation in the Self-Concept," in *The Self: Interdisciplinary Approaches*, edited by J. Strauss and G. Goethals (New York: Springer-Verlag, 1991), pp. 18–48.

Pages 33–34: Peggy Miller and Lois Sperry, "Early Talk about the Past: The Origins of Conversational Stories of Personal Experience," *Journal of Child Language*, **15** (1988), 293–315.

Page 36: I first presented these data at the biennial meeting of the Society for Research in Child Development, in Washington, D.C., April 1997. The study was titled "Trial Balloons: How Children First Exchange Autobiographical Information with One Another."

Page 37: Erving Goffman, *The Presentation of Self in Everyday Life* (New York: Doubleday, 1959).

Page 38: The story on Barry Sonnenfeld and his mother appeared in the *New York Times,* July 11, 1997, p. C1.

Page 41: This excellent book by Brad Shore is called *Culture in Mind* (New York: Oxford University Press, 1996). The quotations appear on pages 375 and 379, respectively.

Page 42: The quotation is from the philosopher Paul Ricouer, *Hermeneutics and the Human Sciences* (Cambridge: Cambridge University Press, 1981).

Page 43: I am talking here about unintended distortions where the rememberer absolutely believes what he or she is recalling. Deliberate lying is another matter. Interesting speculations on the differences can be found in Sissela Bok, *Lying: Moral Choices in Public and Private Life* (New York: Pantheon, 1978).

Page 44: Anthony Greenwald lays out the ways in which the ego dominates our memory process in his article "Totalitarian Ego," *American Psychology,* 35 (1980), 603–618.

Jane Austen, *Emma* (New York: Dutton, 1908).

Pages 44–45: The classic on cognitive dissonance is Leon Festinger's A *Theory of Cognitive Dissonance* (Palo Alto, CA: Stanford University Press, 1956). Elliot Aronson's reformulation of the theory is described in the chapter on self-justification in *The Social Animal,* 7th ed. (New York: W. H. Freeman, 1995).

Page 45: George Eliot, *Middlemarch* (New York: Penguin Classics, 1994). Quotations are from pages 161 and 171, respectively.

Page 46: The study is described in Willem Wagenaar, "Is Memory Self-Serving?" in *The Remembering Self,* edited by Ulric Neisser and Robyn Fivush (New York: Cambridge University Press, 1994).

Page 47: Shelley Taylor, *Positive Illusions* (New York: Basic Books, 1989).

George R. Goethals and Richard Reckman, "Recalling Previously Held Attitudes," in *Memory Observed,* edited by Ulric Neisser (New York: W. H. Freeman, 1991).

Page 48: Michael Ross and Michael Conway, "Remembering One's Past: The Construction of Personal Histories," in *The Handbook of Motivation and Cognition,* edited by Richard Sorrentino and E. Tory Hissons (New York: Guilford Press, 1990).

See Saul M. Kassin and Katherine L. Kiechel, "The Social Psychology of False Confessions: Compliance, Internalization and Confabulation," *Psychological Science,* 7(3) (May 1996), 125–128.

Page 49: See Lawrence Wright's vivid account, *Remembering Satan* (New York: Knopf, 1994).

Page 50: Lee Ross and Richard Nisbett, *The Person and the Situation: Perspectives of Social Psychology* (New York: McGraw-Hill, 1991).

CHAPTER 3: COURTROOMS AND THERAPY ROOMS
Page 56: *Memory Observed,* edited by Ulric Neisser (New York: W. H. Freeman, 1991).

Virginia Woolf, *Moments of Being* (New York: Harcourt Brace Jovanovich, 1985).

Page 57: Ann Brown, "The Development of Memory: Knowing, Knowing about Knowing and Knowing How to Know," in *Advances in Child Development and Behavior*, Vol. 10, edited by H. W. Reese (New York: Academic Press, 1975).

Page 59: Lenore Terr, *Unchained Memories* (New York: Basic Books, 1994).

Page 60: These minutes are taken from a court case heard in the Commonwealth of Massachusetts, 1992.

Page 66: This paper, a classic in which John Dean's testimony about Watergate is compared to the subsequently discovered recordings of those conversations, can be found in *Memory Observed*, edited by Ulric Neisser (New York: W. H. Freeman, 1991).

Page 68: From Sigmund Freud's description of Emmy von XI, in *Standard Edition of the Complete Works of Sigmund Freud*, Vol. II, *Studies on Hysteria*, edited by James Strachey (London: Hogarth Press, 1966).

See Roy Schafer, *Retelling a Life* (New York: Basic Books, 1992). More recently I heard these ideas amplified in a talk Schafer gave at Austen-Riggs Center in Stockbridge, Mass., June 1998.

Two good accounts of James Pennebaker's work can be found in "Confession, Inhibition and Disease," in *Advances in Experimental Social Psychology*, Vol. 22, edited by L. Berkowitz (New York: Academic Press, 1989), pp. 211–244; and "Writing about Emotional Experiences as a Therapeutic Process," *Psychological Science*, 8(3) (May 1997), 162–166.

Page 69: Donald Spence, *Narrative Truth and Historical Truth* (New York: W. W. Norton, 1991).

Page 70: See "Six Roses ou Cirrhose?" in Janet Malcolm, *The Purloined Clinic* (New York: Knopf, 1992), a collection of essays about psychotherapy.

This passage comes from the novel by Daniel Menaker, *The Treatment* (New York: Knopf, 1998), pp. 5–6.

Page 71: These ideas are articulated in Jerome Bruner, "The Autobiographical Process," in *The Culture of Autobiography*, edited by Robert Folkenflik (Palo Alto, CA: Stanford University Press, 1993).

Page 72: Ethel Person, M.D., and Howard Klar, M.D., "Establishing Trauma: The Difficulty Distinguishing between Memories and Fantasies," *Journal of the American Psychoanalytic Association*, 42(4) (1993), 1055–1081. The quotation is from p. 1062.

Page 73: L. Josephs, quoted in Person and Klar, "Establishing Trauma."

Page 75: See Salvatore Minuchin, *Psychosomatic Families* (Cambridge, MA: Harvard University Press, 1978).

Page 76: This passage is found in H. Charles Fishman, *Treating Troubled Adolescents* (New York: Basic Books, 1988), pp. 171–172.

Page 78: The case study here is also from Fishman, *Treating Troubled Adolescents*.

CHAPTER 4: THEN AND NOW: CREATING A SELF THROUGH THE PAST

Page 80: The quotation is from Omar Cabezas, *Fire from the Mountains* (New York: Crown, 1985), p. 205, an account of the Sandinista revolution.

Page 81: Three good and fairly current books about the relationship between recollection and the self are *Remembering Our Past: Studies in Autobiographical Memory,* edited by David Rubin (New York: Cambridge University Press, 1996); Bruce Ross, *Remembering the Personal Past* (New York: Oxford University Press, 1991); and Jefferson Singer and Peter Salovey, *The Remembered Self: Emotion and Memory in Personality* (New York: Free Press, 1993).

Pages 81–82: Natalia Ginzburg, *Family Sayings* (Manchester: Cachet Press, 1984), p. 19.

Page 82: Binjamin Wilkomirski, *Fragments* (New York: Schocken Books, 1995).

   For an account of the Wilkomirski case, see Doreen Carvajal, *New York Times,* November 3, 1998, p. B1.

Pages 82–83: See Daniel Albright, "Literary and Psychological Modes of the Self," in *The Remembering Self,* edited by Ulric Neisser and Robyn Fivush (New York: Cambridge University Press, 1994). The quotation is from page 19.

Page 85: An excellent book that contains descriptions of studies of how people remember is Sylvia Scribner and Michael Cole, *The Psychology of Literacy* (Cambridge, MA: Harvard University Press, 1981).

Pages 85–86: See Ulric Neisser, "Five Kinds of Self-Knowledge," *Philosophical Psychology,* **1** (1988), 35–59.

Page 86: See William James, "The Self," in *Principles of Psychology, The Briefer Course* (New York: Henry Holt, 1892).

   The quotation is from page 1 of Penelope Lively's memoir, *Oleander, Jacaranda: A Childhood Perceived* (New York: HarperCollins, 1994).

Page 88: In addition to autobiographical memory, there is a growing body of work on life stories and what is called the narrative approach to psychology. Two examples are Charlotte Linde, *Life Stories* (New York: Oxford University Press, 1993); and *The Narrative Study of Lives,* edited by Ruthellen Josselson and Amia Liebrlich (London: Sage Publications, 1993).

   The recent exchange between and about the writers Paul Theroux and V. S. Naipaul is an example of people re-creating themselves. Theroux's *Sir Vidia's Shadow* (Boston: Houghton Mifflin, 1998) contains his perspective of this exchange.

Page 89: Erving Goffman, *The Presentation of Self in Everyday Life* (New York: Anchor, 1959).

Pages 90–91: Jon Krakauer, *Into Thin Air* (New York: Willard, 1997).

Page 91: Robert Jay Lifton, *The Nazi Doctors* (New York: Basic Books, 1986).

   Anthony Greenwald, "The Totalitarian Ego: Fabrication and Revision of Personal History," *American Psychologist,* no. 35 (1980), 603–618, is a classic paper on the way in which we distort the past to maintain a good sense of self.

Page 93: Another excellent book on the way in which the mind creates a personal past is Michael Gazzaniga, *The Mind's Past* (San Francisco: University of California Press, 1998).

Jorge Luis Borges, "All Our Yesterdays," translated by Robert Mezey, *New York Review of Books* (December 1995).

Pages 93–94: From Judith Sensibar, "Writing Loss in a Racialized Culture," paper presented at the 1996 annual meeting of the American Psychological Association, Toronto, August 1996.

Page 94: There is an excellent selection on screen memories in Peter Gay, *The Freud Reader* (New York: W. W. Norton, 1989), p. 117.

Page 97: The quotation is from *The New Yorker,* July 8, 1996, p. 55. It is excerpted from Suzannah Lessard, *The Architect of Desire* (New York: Dell, 1997).

Page 99: Jill Ker Conway, *The Road from Coorain* (New York: Knopf, 1989).
Eva Hoffman, *Lost in Translation* (New York: Penguin, 1989), p. 106.
Sharon Olds, "The Lisp," in *The Well Spring* (New York: Knopf, 1996).

Page 100: Grace Paley, "A Conversation with My Father," in *Enormous Changes at the Last Minute* (New York: Farrar, Straus & Giroux, 1960), p. 161.

Pages 100–101: Russell Baker's essay can be found in William Zinsser, *Inventing the Truth: The Art and Craft of Memoir* (Boston: Houghton Mifflin, 1995).

Page 101: Annie Dillard's essay "To Fashion a Text," also in Zinsser's, *Inventing the Truth.*

Pages 102–103: Nadine Gordimer, "Adam's Rib," *The New York Review of Book,* October 5, 1995. The quotation is from page 29.

Page 104: Henry Louis Gates, *13 Ways of Looking at a Black Man* (New York: Random House, 1997).

Page 105: Henry James, *The Wings of the Dove* (New York: Penguin, 1965).

Page 107: Verlyn Klinkenborg, "Playing Shepherd to the Wind," *Double Take,* Summer 1996, p. 72.

CHAPTER 5: REMEMBERING IN PRINT

Page 109: The quotation is from J. D. Salinger, *Seymour, An Introduction* (Boston: Little, Brown, 1955), p. 178.

Page 111: Leo Tolstoy, *Childhood, Boyhood and Youth* (Baltimore: Penguin, 1964); and Virginia Woolf, *Moments of Being* (New York: Harcourt Brace Jovanovich, 1985).
Vladimir Nabokov, *Speak, Memory* (New York: Vintage, 1947).

Page 116: A good paper on gender differences is Robyn Fivush, "Gender and Emotion in Mother-Child Conversations about the Past," *Journal of Narrative and Life History,* 1 (1991), 325–341.

Pages 116–117: Kate Simon, *Bronx Primitive* (New York: Harper & Row, 1982).

Page 117: Art Spiegelman, *Maus—A Survivor's Tale* (New York: Pantheon, 1986).

Pages 117–118: Elias Canetti, *Kafka's Other Trial* (New York: Schocken Books, 1974). The quotation is from pages 12–13.

Page 118: William Zinsser, *Inventing the Truth* (Boston: Houghton Mifflin, 1995).

Page 119: The quotation is from page 79 of Canetti's *Kafka's Other Trial.*

Pages 119–120: St. Augustine, *Confessions,* translated by Henry Chadwick (New York: Oxford University Press, 1991). An excellent selection of Augustine's confessions can be found in *The Oxford Book of Memory,* edited by James McConkey (New York: Oxford University Press, 1996). McConkey's volume contains many excellent excerpts, both fiction and nonfiction, that deal with autobiographical writing.

Page 120: William Wordsworth, *The Poems of William Wordsworth* (Boston: Houghton Mifflin, 1923), p. 106.

Peter Gay, *The Naked Heart* (New York: W. W. Norton, 1995).

See Elias Canetti's autobiography, *The Tongue Set Free* (New York: Farrar, Straus & Giroux, 1979), p. 1.

Page 121: This account of acute depression can be found in Andrew Solomon, "Anatomy of Melancholy," *The New Yorker,* January 12, 1998, p. 46

Page 123: Carrie Young, *Nothing to Do but Stay: My Pioneer Mother* (Ames: University of Iowa Press, 1991).

Page 124: Frederick Douglass, *The Narrative of the Life, My Bondage and Freedom,* and *Life and Times* (published as one volume) (New York: Library of America, 1994).

Page 125 ff: The quotations are from Douglass's one-volume biography, pp. 15, 37, 35, and 18, respectively.

Page 126: A full discussion of this research can be found in *Narratives from the Crib,* edited by Katherine Nelson (Cambridge, MA: Harvard University Press, 1989).

Page 129: John Krystal's ideas are presented in *Memory Distortions,* edited by Daniel Schacter (Cambridge, MA: Harvard University Press, 1995).

Page 130: A good discussion of mechanisms of accuracy and distortion is in an article by Larry Squire, part of a collection of first-rate papers on current theory and research in the ways in which memories are constructed by the brain. See *Memory Distortions,* edited by Daniel Schacter (Cambridge, MA: Harvard University Press, 1995), p. 155.

Page 131: Philip Roth, *Portnoy's Complaint* (New York: Random House, 1969); *The Facts* (New York: Vintage Books, 1988).

Page 132: The two quotations are from Roth's *The Facts,* pp. 129 and 181–182, respectively.

Page 133: *The Narrative Study of Lives,* edited by Ruthellen Josselson and Amia Liebrlich (London: Sage Publications, 1993).

Page 133: Jamaica Kincaid, *My Brother* (New York: Farrar, Straus & Giroux, 1997).

Jerome Bruner's essay "Monologue as Narrative Recreation of the World" was written with Joan Lucariello, and appears in *Narratives from the Crib,* edited by Katherine Nelson (Cambridge, MA: Harvard University Press, 1989).

James Pennebaker, "Confession, Inhibition and Disease," in *Advances in Experimental Social Psychology,* Vol. 22, edited by L. Berkowitz (New York:

Academic Press, 1989), 211–244; "Writing about Emotional Experiences as a Therapeutic Process," *Psychological Science,* 8(3) (May 1997), 162–166.

Pages 134–135: The quotations are from Kincaid's *My Brother,* pp. 17 and 191, respectively.

Page 135: Jamaica Kincaid, *Autobiography of My Mother* (New York: Plume, 1996).

Larry Squire describes the phenomenon of source amnesia in *Memory Distortions,* edited by Daniel Schacter (Cambridge, MA: Harvard University Press, 1995), p. 155.

Page 136: Sue Halpern, "The Awful Truth," *The New York Review of Books,* September 25, 1997, pp. 13–15, discusses the recent surge of memoir writing, specifically the work of writers who use the same material for novels and for nonfiction.

Jerome Bruner, personal correspondence.

Page 138: Primo Levi, *Survival at Auschwitz* (New York: Touchstone Press, 1996).

Page 139: Ingmar Bergman, *The Best Intentions* (New York: Arcade, 1991).

Pages 140–141: Mary Karr, *The Liars' Club* (New York: Viking Press, 1995). The quotations are from pp. 244 and 9, respectively.

Pages 141–142: Kathryn Harrison, *The Kiss* (New York: Random House, 1997).

Page 142: See page 152 in Kincaid's *My Brother.*

Page 143: Frank McCourt, *Angela's Ashes* (New York: Scribner, 1996).

Page 144: Eva Hoffman, *Lost in Translation* (New York: Penguin, 1989), p. 107.

CHAPTER 6: LAYING CLAIM TO THE PAST: WHEN MEMORIES
         BECOME HISTORY

Page 147: Janet Malcolm, *The Purloined Clinic* (New York: Knopf, 1992), p. 118

Page 147: This is presented as fiction, but reads and is talked about as if it were a memoir of living in hiding during World War II. Louis Begley, *Wartime Lies* (New York: Fawcett Columbine, 1991).

Page 148: This theory is most compellingly articulated in the now classic book by the Soviet psychologist Lev Vygotsky, *Language and Thought* (Cambridge, MA: MIT Press, 1962).

See essays by Roger Brown, James Kulik, and Ulric Neisser in *Memory Observed,* edited by Ulric Neisser (New York: W. H. Freeman, 1991).

Page 149: The quotation is from Ellis Cose, *Color Blind: Seeing Beyond Race in a Race-Obsessed World* (New York: HarperCollins, 1997), p. xiii.

Tobias Wolff wrote the earlier memoir of his childhood, *This Boy's Life* (New York: Atlantic Monthly Press, 1989). A year later, his brother published a memoir of his childhood: Geoffrey Wolff, *The Duke of Deception, Memories of My Father* (New York: Vintage, 1990).

James Thurber, "A Curb in the Sky," in *Thurber Carnival* (New York: Dell, 1964).

Page 151: Nicholas Kristof, *New York Times,* January 22, 1997, p. A1.

Page 152: Willem Waagenar, "Is Memory Self Serving?" In *The Remembering Self,* edited by Ulric Neisser and Robyn Fivush (Cambridge: Cambridge University Press, 1994).

Pages 154–155: The quotations here and on pages 155 and 155–156 are from Tom Segev's comprehensive look at the plight of Jews in Israel after World War II, *The Seventh Million* (New York: Hill and Wang, 1993), pp. 447, 452, and 477, respectively.

Page 156: From a paper by Stanley Greenspan. In *Storied Lives,* edited by George C. Rosenwald and Richard L. Ochberg (New Haven, CT: Yale University Press, 1992), pp. 154 and 150.

Page 157: *Maus—A Survivor's Tale* (New York: Pantheon, 1986) is an extraordinary two-volume memoir of the cartoonist Art Spiegelman's father's experiences in a concentration camp. The memoir is presented as a book-length cartoon and contains the relationship between author and his father, as well as a presentation of the father's account of his past.

Page 157: See Elie Wiesel, *Night* (New York: Hill and Wang, 1960).

Page 158: M. M. Bakhtin, *Problems of Dostoekvsky's Poetics* (Minneapolis: University of Minnesota Press, 1984).

The quotation on this page and page 159 is from the anonymously presented comments and essays in "Talk of the Town," *The New Yorker,* April 1997.

Page 159: Daniel Wegner, "Transactive Memory: A Contemporary Analysis of the Group Mind." In *Theories of Group Behavior,* edited by Brian Mullen and George R. Goethals (New York: Springer-Verlag, 1987).

Page 161: Tim O'Brien, in *The Things They Carried* (New York: Penguin, 1990), writes about the nature of memory and fiction as well as describing in vivid detail what it was like to fight as a member of the United States Army during the Vietnam War. The quotation is from p. 40.

Pages 161–162: Robert McNamara, *In Retrospect* (New York: Vintage, 1995).

Pages 165–166: *New York Times,* February 1, 1998, sec. 4, p. 4.

Page 166: Frederic C. Bartlett, *Remembering* (New York: Cambridge University Press, 1932), is a great classic on the subject of remembering, and the power of groups in shaping memories.

Page 167: The article on the Mesopotamian cylinders appeared in the *New York Times,* March 1, 1998, sec. 4, p. 14.

Page 168: The two quotations are from the *New York Times,* March 2, 1998, p. A6.

# INDEX

Abelson, Robert, 28
accuracy, expectations of, 50
Albright, Daniel, 82–83
Albright, Madeleine, 156
amnesia, source, 15–16, 135
*Angela's Ashes* (McCourt), 143
*Anna Karenina* (Tolstoy), 25–26
Aronson, Elliot, 45, 167
artifacts, and reconstructing
    historical events, 150–151
Asian cultures, 32–33, 128
    and recall, 50–51
attunement, 26
audience, for the past, 154–159
Augustine, 119–120
autobiographical information, 26
autobiographical memory, 9, 22,
    27, 85, 92, 103
    and family therapy, 78
    first signs of, 27–30, 86
    and historical knowledge,
        151–152
    and level of focus, 124
    and narrative skills, 30–31

autobiographical recall, 17–18
autobiographical stance, 114–119
autobiographical talk, 27, 30
autobiographical thinking, 26
autobiography, 11–12
    culture of, 119–124
    developmental origins of,
        109–116
    distinction from memoir,
        100–101
    motivations for writing,
        122–145
    reader's role in, 136–141
    and re-creating self, 88–89
    and remembered self, 88–89
    and the self as personal historian,
        83–86
*Autobiography of My Mother*
    (Kincaid), 135

babies, and memory, 27–28
Baker, Russell, 100–101
Bakhtin, Mikhail, 158

Bartlett, Frederic C., 166, 167
basal ganglia, effects of damage to, 4
Begley, Louis, 146–147
Bergman, Ingmar, 139
blank page method of lying, 77–78
Borges, Jorge Luis, 93
borrowed memory, 157–159
Bowlby, John, 27
brain
    and language, 121
    and memory, 5
Brown, Ann, 9, 57
Brown, Roger, 148
Broyard, Anatole, 104–107
Bruner, Jerome, 36, 71, 82, 119,
    133, 136–137
Buñuel, Luis, 13, 14

Cambodia, 128
Canetti, Elias, 117–120, 133
categories, and recall, 6
children
    and autobiographical memory,
        29–30
    conversation partners and mem-
        ory, 37–38
    developmental origins of autobi-
        ography, 109–116
    early autobiographical references,
        86
    early remembering behavior,
        27–30
    influence of friends on memories,
        35–37
    influencing memories of, 32–35
    language and memory, 30–32
    life stories, 114–115
    parent-child talk, 33–34
    remembering processes, 84–86
Chinese
    and behavior attribution, 50
    children's memory capacity, 33
chronological memory, 100–102
Clinton, Bill, 163–167
cognitive dissonance theory, 44–47,
    90–92

Cole, Michael, 85
collective memories, 148
conflict, in a shared past, 37–40,
    42–43
consensual truth, 14
consequences, of memory, 58
consistency, 47–48
consistent self, 90, 92
constraint, in recall, 58
context (of remembering), 124
    for autobiography, 124
    and connecting past and present
        selves, 87
    and Holocaust memories,
        156–157
    and testimony, 65
continuity, and memory as chronol-
    ogy, 100–102
conversation
    with friends as context for re-
        membering, 124
    memories created in, 24–51
Conway, Jill Ker, 99, 102
Conway, Michael, 48
cooling function of narrative, 133
Cose, Ellis, 148–149
courtroom, as setting for remem-
    bering, 52–53, 56–67, 79
Creeley, Robert, 136
cultures, and shaping of minds, 42

daydreams, 135
Dean, John, 66
Dillard, Annie, 101, 102
direct lie method, 77
disagreement, and family therapy,
    76, 77
disguise, as motivation for writing
    autobiography, 131–133
dissonance. See cognitive disso-
    nance theory
dissonance reduction, 45, 90–91
distortion (of memories), 45–49
    by court witnesses, 57
    and lying, 104
    mechanisms of, 43, 45–51

distortion (*cont.*)
    of old views, 48
    and recall of shared experiences,
        43–44
Douglass, Frederick, 124–130

Eastern cultures, and self-concepts,
    33
Eliot, George, 45
episodic memory, 7, 66
events
    dissimilar memories of, 160–162
    *See also* historical events; shared
        events
events, significant
    general view and personal view
        of, 149–150
    and others' memories, 151–154
    and recall, 56
everyday life, memory of, 97–99
experiences
    ordering of. *See* scripts
    transforming by articulating,
        68–69
    value of articulating, 68–69
extended self, 85–86
externalized memory, news articles
    as, 163

face (self-representation), 89–91
*Facts, The* (Roth), 130–133
family therapy, 75–78
fantasy
    disentangling from reality,
        72–74
    repression of, 49
Faulkner, William, 93–95
Festinger, Leon, 44
fiction, and creative recollection,
    102–104
Franklin, George, 59
Franklin-Lipsker, Eileen, 59
Freud, Sigmund, 26, 68, 70, 72, 73,
    75, 94
Freudian analysts, 71, 72

friends
    conversations with as context for
        remembering, 124
    influence on each other's memo-
        ries, 35–37
    and remembering, 40–41
Fritsch, Jane, 165

Gandhi, Mahatma, 168
Gates, Henry Louis, 104
Gay, Peter, 21, 120
Gingrich, Newt, 148
Ginzburg, Natalia, 81–82
Godse, Gopal, 168
Goethals, George, 47
Goffman, Erving, 37, 39, 89, 92
Greenspan, Henry, 156
Greenwald, Anthony, 44, 91

Halpern, Sue, 136
Han, Jessica, 32–33
Harris, Andy, 91
Harrison, Kathryn, 14, 141–143
Hill, Anita, 163
hindsight, 126
hippocampus, effects of damage
    to, 4
historical events
    personal and public memory of,
        163
    perspectives of, 159–163, 168
    reconstructing, 150–151
historical memory
    convergence with personal mem-
        ory, 146–154
    creating, 163–169
historical truth, 69
history
    and other people's memories,
        147, 154–159
    when memories become,
        146–169
Hoffman, Eva, 99, 144–145
Holocaust, memories of, 13, 150,
    154–159

Holocaust Memorial Museum
(Washington, D.C.), 157
hysterical blindness, 128

illusions, positive, 18
imagining, 5
impacts, positive, 68
infants
and memory, 28
mother-infant relationships,
26–27
influence, on others' memories,
49–50
Ingram, Paul, 49–50
input stage of memory, 5
interactions
and family therapy, 75, 76
See also conversation
internal memory, 59
intimacy
mother-infant relationship, 26
remembering as an act of, 24–26
Isikoff, William, 164

James, Henry, 105, 119
James, William, 86
Jones, Paula, 164
Josephs, L., 73
Josselson, Ruth Ellen, 133
Joyce, James, 119
judge, role of in courtroom, 60–65
jury instructions, 60–65

Kafka, Franz, 117–119
Karr, Mary, 12, 139–141, 144
Kassin, Saul, 48
Khmer Rouge, 128
Kincaid, Jamaica, 133–136, 142
King, Martin Luther, Jr., 148–149
Kiss, The (Harrison), 141–142
Kitiyama, Shinobu, 33
Klar, Howard, 72–74
Klinkenborg, Verlyn, 107
knowledge. See semantic memory

Koreans
children's memory capacity, 33
and references to past, 32–33
Krakauer, John, 90
Krystal, John, 129
Kulik, James, 148

Labov, William, 169
language
brain and, 121
and reminiscences of children,
30–32
Leichtman, Michelle, 32–33
Levi, Primo, 102, 138, 144
Lewinsky, Monica, 163–166
Lewontin, Richard, 10
life story
of children, 114–115
and chronology, 100, 102
and remembered self, 88
See also autobiography
Lifton, Robert Jay, 91
line, maintaining a, 37
Lively, Penelope, 11, 86
Loftus, Elizabeth, 17, 31
long-term memory, 7–8
lying, 104–105
blank page method of, 77–78
direct lie method, 77

McCourt, Frank, 143
McNamara, Robert, 161–162
Malcolm, Janet, 70, 146–147, 150
manifestation, 9–10
Mann, Thomas, 119
Markus, Hazel, 33
memoir, distinction from autobiography, 100–101
memorials, and others' memories,
154, 155
memories
accuracy and vividness of, 15
borrowing, 158, 159
collective, 148
created in conversation, 24–51

memories (*cont.*)

    as history, 146–169

    influence of others on, 35–37, 49–50

    influencing children's, 32–35

    negative, 46

    overlapping, 149

    painful, 129

    positive, 46

    repressed, 5, 97, 156

    shared, 81, 159–160, 164–166

    short-term, 7–8

    spoken, 54

    suppressed, 156–157

    traumatic 5

    vivid, 5

    vulnerability to suggestion, 49

memory

    borrowed, 157–159

    capacity expansion during childhood, 84–86

    as chronology, 100–102

    consequences of, 58

    and constructing self, 89

    in courtrooms, 58–67

    developmental origins of, 27

    distortions of, 45–48

    episodic, 7, 66

    externalized, 163

    historical, 146–154, 163–169

    influence of others on, 8, 48

    language and children's reminiscences, 30–32

    layers of, 5, 130

    long-term, 7–8

    and narrative, 71–72

    personal and historical, 146–154

    processes of, 4, 8

    public form of, 12–14, 16–19, 67

    recognition, 27–28

    and recollection, 3

    repisodic, 66

    representataive, 127

    screen, 94–95

    selective, 88–89

    semantic, 7

    stages of, 5–6

    as template, 21, 88, 93–97

    and therapy, 67–79

    transactional and transactive, 160–162

    unspoken, 155

    vicarious, 150

memory, theory of

    instructions to juries as, 60–65

memory tasks, organizing strategies, 85

Menaker, Daniel, 70

mental experience, communicating, 69–70

meta-memory, 9, 57, 85

metamir, 102, 103

Miller, Peggy, 19, 33–34

Minuchin, Salvatore, 75

mood, and recall, 8

mother-infant relationships, 26–27

motivated omissions, 106

motivation, for writing autobiographies, 122–145

Mullen, Mary, 32–33

narrative

    cooling function of, 133

    and memory, 71–72

    and therapy, 74, 75

    *See also* writing

narrative truth, 14, 15, 69

narratives, psychology of, 71

negative memories, 46

Neisser, Ulric, 15, 17, 56, 85, 148

Nelson, Katherine, 28–29

neural pathways, for memories, 5

newspapers, and creating historical memory, 163–166

Nisbett, Richard, 50

nondisclosure, 104–105

O'Brien, Tim, 161, 162

Ofshe, Richard, 49

Olds, Sharon, 99

omissions, in recalling the past,
     104–107
organizing strategies, and memory
     tasks, 85
output stage of memory. *See* re-
     trieval stage of memory
overestimation, 47
overlapping memories, 149

painful memories, 129
Paley, Grace, 100
parent-child talk, as shared remem-
     bering, 33–34
parents
     influencing children's memories,
          32–35
     recounting the past to toddlers,
          29
     and shared remembering with
          toddlers, 34
past
     construction of in psychoanalytic
          settings, 74
     creating a self through the,
          80–108
     disagreement about, 50–51
     finding an audience for,
          154–159
     relating to present, 20
     self as center of the, 44–51
     use of to illuminate the present,
          75
     when memories become history,
          146–169
past self, and present self, 81–108
patient-therapist relationship, 70
peeking, 143–145
Pennebaker, James, 68, 133–134
Person, Ethel, 72–73, 74
perspectives
     converging, 159–163
     of historical events, 159–163,
          168
persuasion, as motivation for writ-
     ing autobiography, 124–130
phenylketonuria (PKU), 10

Porada, Edith, 167
*Portnoy's Complaint* (Roth), 130
positive illusions, 18
positive impacts, of putting past
     into words, 68
positive memories, 46
positive self-concepts
     recalling exceptions to, 152
posttraumatic stress syndrome, 129
present self, and past self, 81–108
Prok, Andrus, 77
psychoanalysis, 69
psychologists, goals of, 83
public memory, 12–14
     in courtrooms, 67
     and disagreement, 18–19
     and shaping private memory,
          16–18
public transactions, and remember-
     ing, 9

reality, disentangling from fantasy,
     72–74
recall, 5, 57
     and categories, 6
     constraint in, 58
     frequency of, 8
     self-awareness of, 58
Reckman, Richard, 47
recognition memory
     in babies, 27–28
recollection, 3, 4
     creative, 102
recounting
     and autobiographical writing,
          118
rehearsal (repetition of recollec-
     tion), 8, 56
remembered self, 93, 107–108
     and remembering self, 86–89
remembering
     as an act of intimacy, 24–26
     collaborative, and therapy,
          67–79
     consequences of, 21–22
     with friends, 40–41

remembering (*cont.*)
  motivation for and social context, 9
  sequence of, 5
  and settings, 52–53
  shared, 33–34
  of witnesses, 57, 64–66
  in writing, 109–145
  *See also* recall; retrieval
remembering self, 93, 107–108
  and remembered self, 86–89
reminiscences
  and autobiographical writing, 110, 118
  of children, 30–32
repisodic memory, 66
representative memory, 127
repressed memories, 5, 97, 156
repression, of fantasy, 49
retrieval stage of memory, 6–7, 56
Ricouer, Paul, 42
Rilke, Rainer Maria, 24
roles
  in a courtroom, 60–63
  in spoken memories, 54
Ross, Lee, 50
Ross, Michael, 48
Roth, Philip, 131–135

Salinger, J. D., 142, 145
Schacter, Daniel, 4, 151
Schafer, Roy, 68, 69
Schank, Roger, 28
Schwartz, Delmore, 3
screen memory, 94–95
Scribner, Sylvia, 85
scripts, 28–29
Segev, Tom, 13, 154–155
selective memory, and self-creation, 88–89
self
  as center of the past, 44–51
  creating through memories, 80–108
  extended, 85–86
  for others, 89–93

as personal historian, 82–86
  for self, 89–93
  subjective, 120
  *See also* past self; present self; remembered self; remembering self
self-awareness, of recall, 58
self-concept, 90–91
  and chronological memory, 101
  positive, and recalling exceptions to, 152
  variation across cultures, 33
self-creation, through selective memory, 88–89
self-deception, 47
self-presentation (face), 89–91
  and omissions, 106
self re-creation, 92
semantic memory, 7
Sensibar, Judith, 93–95
settings
  court proceedings, 52–53, 56–57, 79
  and life stories, 107
  and remembering, 52–53
  therapy, 67–79
shared events
  distorted recall of, 43–44
  and recollection of, 41–42
shared history, 148
shared memories, 159–160, 166
  and constructing a self, 81
  historically significant, 164–165
Shore, Brad, 41–42
short-term memory, 7–8
siblings, and different recollections, 15, 43
Simon, Kate, 116–117
social significance
  and recall, 17
Solomon, Andrew, 121
Sonnenfeld, Barry, 38–39, 42
source amnesia, 15–16, 135
speech
  and development of autobiographical memory, 29
  *See also* language

Spence, Donald, 14, 69, 74
Spiegelman, Art, 117, 157
Squire, Larry, 135
Starr, Kenneth, 163, 164
Stern, Claudio, 10
Stern, Daniel, 26–27
storage stage of memory, 5
story telling, 12
subjective self, 120
suggestibility, and children's memories, 31
suggestion, memories and vulnerability to, 49
suppressed memories, of Holocaust, 156–157

talking. *See* autobiographical talk; conversation
Taylor, Shelley, 18, 47
template memory, 21, 88, 93–97
Terr, Lenore, 59
therapist-patient relationship, 70
    as setting for remembering, 53
therapy
    goal of, 79
    as a setting for remembering, 53, 67–79
Thomas, Clarence, 163
Thurber, James, 149
toddlers
    and memory, 27–29, 84–85
    and shared remembering with parents, 34
    *See also* children
totalitarian ego, 44
transactional memory, 160
transactive memory, 161–162
transference, 70–73, 75, 88
traumatic events, 73, 129
    repressing of, 97
Tripp, Linda, 164, 165
truth
    consensual, 14
    historical, 69
    inventing, 103–104
    narrataive, 14, 15, 69

truth telling, 13–16
Tulving, Endel, 7
*Twelve Angry Men* (film), 55
Tzara, Tristan, 70

uniqueness, of a memory and recall, 8
unspoken memory, 155

vicarious memory, 150
Vidal, Gore, 100
voyeurism, and reading autobiographies, 143
Vygotsky, Lev, 148

Wagenaar, Willem, 46, 152
Waletzky, Joshua, 169
Wang, Qi, 33
Wegner, Daniel, 159–161, 163
Western cultures, and self-concepts, 33
White, Stanford, 97
Whitewater, 164
Wiesel, Elie, 157–158
Wilkomirski, Binjamin, 98
witnesses and remembering, 52, 54–57, 64–66
Wolff, Geoffrey, 149
Wolff, Tobias, 149
Woolf, Virginia, 56, 116, 117
Wordsworth, William, 120
Wright, Lawrence, 49
writers, 83
writing
    autobiographical, 109–145
    and context for autobiography, 124

Yablonsky, Linda, 136
Young, Carrie, 123

Zinsser, William, 103, 118